THE SAVVY EMCEE

HOW TO BE A DYNAMIC MASTER OF CEREMONIES

RAE A. STONEHOUSE

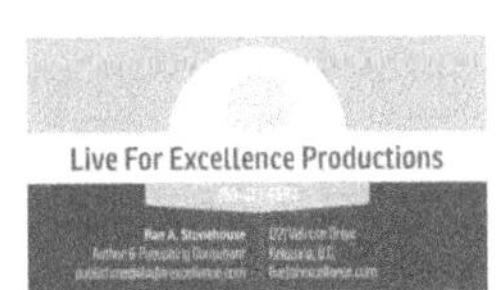

E-book - ISBN: 978-1-9990454-5-6
Paperback - ISBN: 978-1-9990454-6-3

Live For Excellence Productions
1221 Velrose Drive
Kelowna, B.C., Canada
V1X6R7
https://liveforexcellence.com

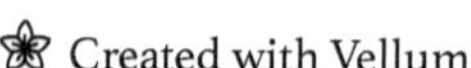 Created with Vellum

CONTENTS

PART III
ADDITIONAL RESOURCES:

1. CONNECT WITH US

S ubscribe to our newsletter to receive sage advice and updates from Rae A. Stonehouse on networking, job searching skills and other self-help professional development training as they become available and receive **52 Power Networking Tips: How to Network Like a Pro**, a free e-book.

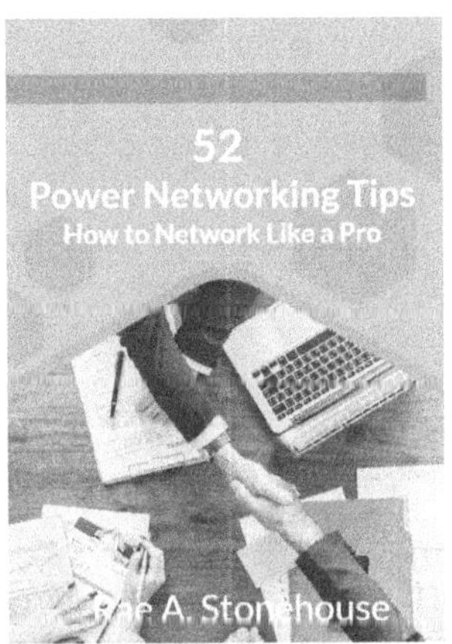

Sign up url BookHip.com/JDGWKZ

. . .

Follow us on Facebook https://www.facebook.com/savveyemcee/

Twitter: https://twitter.com/MisterEmceeRae

And our website https://mremcee.com

INTRODUCTION

Meetings, get-togethers and events are happening every day somewhere near you. And probably right now as you are reading this.

Many will be organized and run effectively. Others will leave audience members saying "Well, that was a waste of time!" Poor organization and a lack of leadership can prevent an organization from achieving its purpose.

Meetings are expensive. From the actual cost of running the event, paying employees to attend and incidental costs such as travel, meals and accommodation all add up.

An experienced, master of ceremonies can ensure an event is run smoothly from start to finish.

There is a need for experienced, self-confident speaking professionals to meet the events and meetings industry requirements.

This book is written to fast-track anyone who wants to learn how to emcee events.

Welcome to **The Savvy Emcee: How to Be a Dynamic Master of Ceremonies.**

The content of this book is derived from my previous book **E=Emcee Squared: Tips & Techniques to Becoming a Dynamic Master of Ceremonies** published in 2014.

This expanded edition will be helpful to those of you who have been thrust into the position of having to emcee an event with short notice and without experience as well as those who are more experienced and are thinking about earning income and perhaps turning their emceeing into a side-hustle or a full-time business.

Later on in the book I delve into public speaking skills development as it is one of the basic skills required to serve as a Master of Ceremonies. You will notice I use the terms master of ceremonies, MC and emcee interchangeably throughout the book.

Before we get started with all the exciting tips and techniques, let me share with you why I created this book in the first place.

My professional career has been as a Registered Nurse working predominantly in mental health and psychiatry. I can't recall there being many if any opportunities to practice my craft of emceeing while working in that capacity. In fact, being an Emcee hasn't even featured on my "bucket list" of things I need to accomplish before I pass on to the afterlife.

You might have noticed I called emceeing a *craft* in the previous paragraph. I truly believe it is. For me, becoming a proficient master of ceremonies developed incrementally while participating in hundreds, if not thousands of weekly Toastmasters meetings.

I joined Toastmasters to develop my public speaking skills. Before joining, I was terrified of standing and speaking before a group, *public speaking* as it is commonly referred to.

I quickly learned public speaking and leadership went hand-in-hand. To be an effective leader, you need to be a good communicator. To be an effective speaker, you need to be a good leader.

The Toastmasters program provided me ample opportunities to

develop my emceeing skills in their weekly meetings as well as outside of the club environment. The weekly club meeting and program provides as many speaking opportunities for its members as can be packed into the amount of time allotted. The different roles, while providing speaking opportunities, also provide varying levels of leadership skill building. The basic leadership skills you learn are readily usable for the more challenging roles you take on.

My journey to becoming an accomplished Toastmaster has included many leadership roles and positions. Each has brought its own challenges and lessons learned. In my early years in Toastmasters I recall being *volunteered* to introduce an Area Governor at a speech contest gathering that was being hosted locally. The Area Governor's role was to officiate at the speech contest, that is, *emcee* the event.

I recall being terrified having to go up onto the stage, with everyone staring at me while I introduced the Area Governor. The very next year... I was the Area Governor!

A lot can happen in a year. I found I actually liked standing on the stage, with all the audience's eyes on me.

Since then I have taken on ever-increasingly challenging leadership roles in Toastmasters such as Division Governor, Lieutenant Governor of Education & Training (LGET), District Governor and Past District Governor.

Outside of Toastmasters I have taken on leadership roles as a Director, then the Chair of a local entrepreneur's society. In that capacity I organized 30 or so Townhall meetings which were panel discussions with local, experienced entrepreneurs discussing issues of importance to those interested in the topic of the meeting.

My role included subject development, speaker recruitment, speaker coaching, marketing and promoting the event, selling registrations, developing the agenda/timeline, moderating the event and providing post event follow-up.

Many of those activities could arguably be described as being an event planner's duties. As an Emcee, I take a proactive approach and don't leave anything to chance.

Throughout this book I provide you with tips and techniques I have learned along the way in becoming an effective Master of Ceremonies and turning it into a business venture. As Mr. Emcee (my business name) I provide master of ceremonies and event organizing services in my local market.

The task of emceeing is very much like the proverbial tip of an iceberg i.e. much of what takes place is behind the scenes where the public doesn't see. Far too many people have the view anyone can walk onto a stage, announce a bunch of names, crack a few jokes and be effective.

Nothing could be further from the truth! As you will see, I share with you the *"behind the scenes"* details needed to be a dynamic Master of Ceremonies.

Throughout this book you will notice I use a *conversational* style of writing. Sure, you don't get to speak back to me but it might be helpful to read the book as if I was coaching you.

This book is written from the perspective that you the reader has a basic concept of what is involved in being a Master of Ceremonies but would like to learn more, so you can do it yourself. An Emceeing for Dummies, if you will. Not that you are a dummy of course...

As in other articles and books I have written, I utilize what I call an *"onion"* approach. In exploring a topic, we peel layer after layer away, so we get to the essence of the subject. Much like peeling back the layers of an onion but hopefully, without all the tears that often accompany doing so. I hope you find this appealing! Okay, that's the only pun I will be using... maybe.

In my first edition of this book, I leveraged Albert Einstein's name recognition with E=MC [squared] and applied it to our topic.

The MC (Emcee) portion should be fairly obvious. But what about the **E** portion of the formula? Drawing from the field of public speaking and leadership, **E** can have multiple meanings (all of which you should be):

- Entertaining
- Educational
- Enthusiastic
- Endearing
- Encouraging
- Effortless
- Economic [of time]
- Efficient
- Early
- Engaging

I could likely pull out my dictionary and overwhelm you with a plethora of words that start with E, so I will stop here.

You will see Albert Einstein throughout this book as I have put him to work in introducing sage advice in our **Tips From the Pros** sections.

One last comment before we get started. While this book provides a systematic approach to serving as a dynamic Emcee, your self-confidence, poise, courage, public speaking skills and courage to take on a role many others would avoid at all costs, will go a long way in ensuring your success.

Those are all factors that are beyond the scope of this book. However, if I can do it... you can too!

Rae Stonehouse a.k.a. Mr. Emcee

PART I

LOGISTICS

2. TAKE CHARGE: THE SUCCESS OF YOUR EVENT DEPENDS UPON YOU!

Yes, the success of any event falls onto the shoulders of everyone who is organizing it. The challenge can be in identifying who actually is in charge? An event, or even a smaller scale meeting can have several key players.

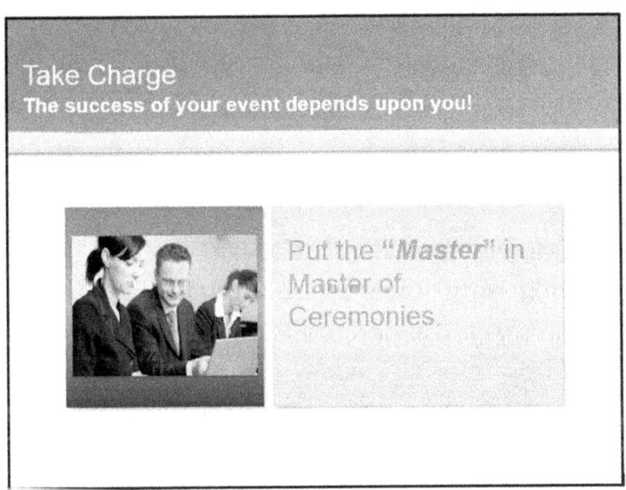

There may be a *Meeting Planner/Organizer* involved.

Likely, the event would have to be larger in scale for them to gain revenue from the venture, however many volunteer their time and expertise to worthy causes. Their role is to oversee the logistics of the entire event.

A larger event can be broken down to smaller mini events. They may engage you to take on the role of emceeing a specific portion of the larger scale event. This can provide challenges for you. More about this later.

You can also have a **client or event sponsor** taking on an active leadership role. While they have a vested interest in the success of the event, after all they are paying for it, they may not have the organizational skills and everything else you bring as a Master of Ceremonies. Their involvement may *not* be helpful.

Taking *charge* does not mean acting as a military general where only you know the *battle plan*. It isn't about issuing orders that must be followed. It is helpful to think of your role as being that of an **orchestra conductor**.

While strategy is necessary, the event goes much smoother if everyone is working from the same page. I don't have a musical background, but I do know the conductor leads the musicians to play from the same page, together and adding to each other's sound. When that doesn't happen... I guess that's what they call Jazz!

A helpful tip is to insist on the client designating a single person to be the **go-to-person** to solve problems. Quite often there can be last-minute changes to the agenda or on-the-spot input that can change the agenda. Simply insist all changes to the agenda and announcements come from the **designated client representative**. That way the client is in control of the meeting and you look good in their eyes.

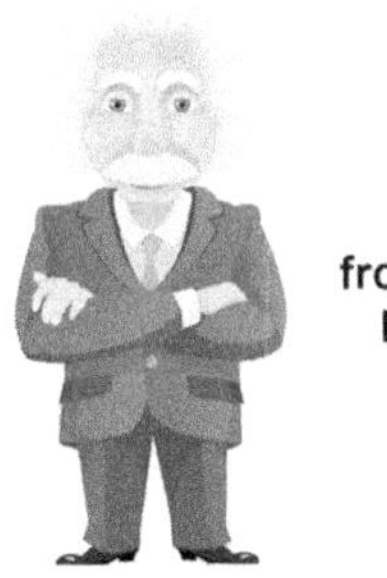

AN EMCEE SHOULD HAVE THE ABILITY TO **"ACE"** AN EVENT.

THE THREE A'S:

- **Awake** - make them laugh and they will pay attention.
- **Alert** - look forward to your next quip.
- **Alive** - even if the speaker you introduce bores them, they will anticipate your return, expecting more fun.

The three C's:

- **Current** - talk about today's news events or this event.
- **Clever** - intellectually funny, not silly.
- **Concise** - say it quickly, make your point, get off.

SHOULD THE CLIENT REQUEST A *SERIOUS* SET OF INTRODUCTIONS THEN you employ...

The three E's:

- **Excitement** - about the person or company.
- **Enthusiasm** - about what they do.
- **Energy** - to keep attention even if the subject is dry.

"The right Emcee can make or break your event. It is important to position yourself as the right person."

Source: Unknown

3. GET ORGANIZED

E vent organizing can be a lot like cat juggling.

As the Emcee your role is to create order from chaos. Quite often your client has an idea about the way they want their event to flow but they really don't know how to make it happen. That's where you come in. I liken emceeing to cat juggling. Metaphorically of course!

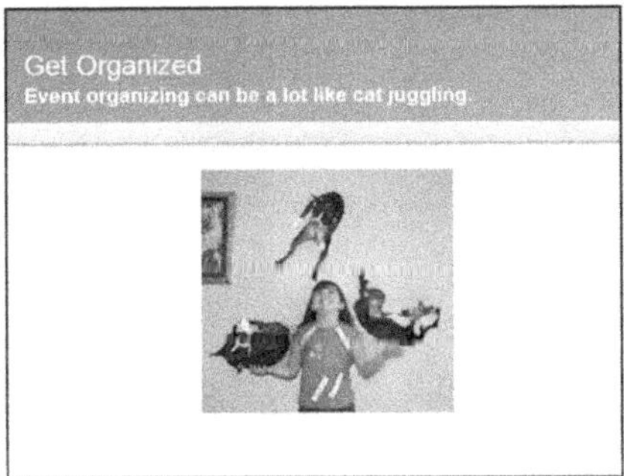

Okay, so they may actually be dogs in the picture above, but I think you get the idea... [I thought they were cats for the longest time.]

Sometimes the cats fly where you want to and sometimes, they have a mind of their own and go where they want to.

Cats are like ideas. Your client likely has lots of them and they are flying all over the place. Your role as Emcee is to get those cats flying in formation i.e. to get all of those ideas to make sense and work together.

4. GETTING ORGANIZED: THINK LOGISTICALLY

Consider all aspects of your event.

The **Five Ws** and an **H** provide the framework for writing any good story. They also serve well to perform a strategic analysis of any event you are organizing. We will break them down to logistical questions you should ask as the *first* step in organizing an event.

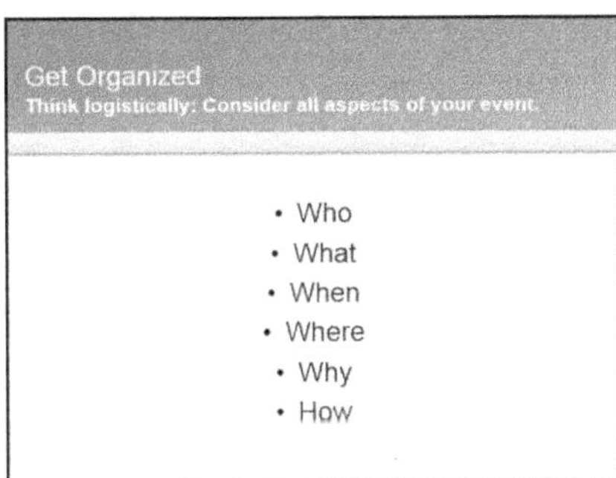

Who:

- Who is the client? Contact info?
- Who do you report to?
- Who do you approach during the event if there is a problem?

- Who will be participating or speaking in the program? Examples: keynote speakers, VIPs, dignitaries (Note: we talk about introducing speakers later and the information you will need to collect from them.)
- Who will be in the audience?

What:

- What is the nature of the event?
- Is the event intended to be educational, informative, entertaining, thought provoking, to provide recognition? Any of the above, or all?
- What does the planned program look like i.e. structure, elements?

When:

- What is the date and time of the event?
- Will you have any duties to perform before or after the actual speaking portion of the event? Example: Meeting & greeting at a pre-meeting reception or post event get-together. Corralling guests from a reception to the main room.
- Are there any plans in place for rescheduling the event if unforeseen and insurmountable challenges occur?

Where:

- What is the location of the event i.e. the street address?
- What specific room will the event be held in at the location?
- Where will you be emceeing from i.e. is there a stage, head table etc.
- Are there any environmental concerns? Example: If your event is outside could weather have an effect on the program i.e. wind, rain, snow etc.

Why:

- What is the purpose of this event? What does the hosting organization hope to achieve? Are there any hidden agendas?

How:

- How will the hosting organization determine whether this event is a success or not?
- How will the hosting organization determine if your participation in the event is a success or not?

Think Logistically: What do you need to know that you don't know but you really should know?

Thinking logistically is very much like being a detective. It can be frustrating to learn a detail that if you had known at the time, it could have saved you a lot of time and effort. This can sometimes result from assumptions people make. "Oh, sorry, I thought you knew that!" On the other hand, there are people who like to control information.

Information can be used as personal power. I'm sure you have heard the term "It's on a need to know basis." You do need to know!

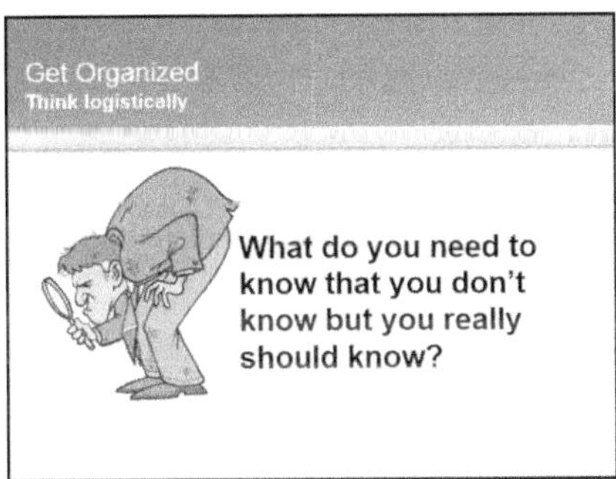

In the previous section we discussed the five Ws and an H. The Ws provide us with information we need to work on the *How* portion of

our event. Given the information we have collected, *how* are we going to make this event work and be successful?

There was a television commercial a few years back, I believe it might have been for Holiday Inn. The commercial used the tagline "***The best surprise is no surprise.***" I keep that tagline in mind when I am organizing an event. I want to know all the details so I can develop an effective plan of action.

By envisioning how each part of the agenda/program would play out, I can determine the logistics related to each portion.

I think in terms of *what* does it look like if it works? What has to take place for it work? What if it doesn't work out and things go wrong? What can I do to resolve the problem at the time and are there any actions I can take to prevent the problem from happening in the first place?

In the next section we discuss how to keep track of the logistics you have identified, on a spreadsheet. At this point, thinking logistically is about identifying factors, conditions or activities that have to take place for something else to go smoothly.

Later in this book we discuss developing a backup plan should something go wrong.

5. GETTING ORGANIZED: DEVELOP AN AGENDA

I t is not that unusual for the event host or organizer to hand you a roughly drawn sequence of events with the comment "Here's your agenda!"

"Good for them I say!" "Now let's make a real one." I'm going to suggest you take their info and develop it into three different documents.

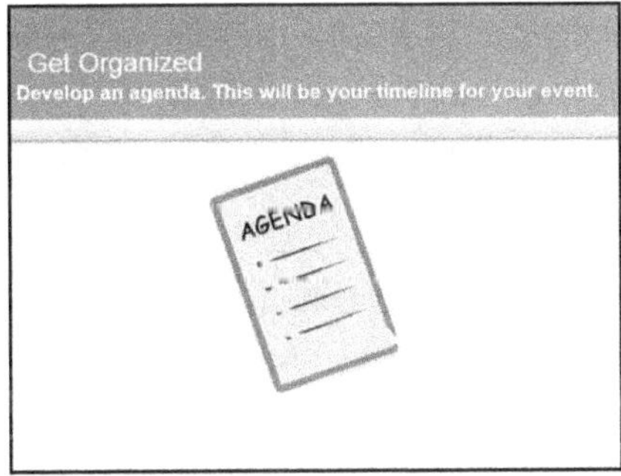

DOCUMENT ONE (MINUTE-BY-MINUTE TIMELINE): THIS IS A TOOL TO allow you to strategically develop a plan of action for your event.

	Time	Time Allotted	Start Time	End Time	Activity	Who?	Logistics	Comments
1	Time	Time Allotted	Start Time	End Time	Activity	Who?	Logistics	Comments
2	6:00	90 min	6:00 PM	7:30 PM	Registration Opens		need cashbox, float, tickets	Joe will bring cashbox + float
3	6:15							
4	6:30							
5	6:35							
6	6:40							
7	6:45		6:45 PM	7:00 PM	Move guests into Hall	Ushers	Need 2 ushers, one for each entrance	
8	6:50							
9	6:55							
10	7:00	3 min	7:00 PM	7:03 PM	Opening & Welcoming Comments	MC		
11	7:03	5 min	7:03	7:08	Comments from Sponsor	Sponsor	Have trophy at lectern/ need sponsor intro	Bill will bring trophy
12	7:08	2 min	7:08	7:10	Introduction of Keynote Speaker	MC	Speaker has provided intro	
13	7:10	50 min	7:10	8:00	Keynote speaker	Keynote		
14	8:00	2 min	8:00	8:02	Thank Keynote & present gift	MC	Have speaker gift behind podium	
15	8:02	2min	8:02	8:04	Welcome to awards ceremony	MC		
16	8:04	2min	8:04	8:06	Introduce Award Ceremony Sponsor	MC		
17	8:06	50 min	8:06	8:56	Awards Ceremony	MC		
18	8:56	4 min	8:56	9:00	Closing Remarks	MC		
19	9:00		9:00		Adjourn			

To do this, you will create a spreadsheet document in Excel. If you don't have a version of Microsoft Office, free versions of spreadsheet software are available on-line through Open Office.

Helpful Tip: if you aren't familiar with how spreadsheets work, *columns* go down, *rows* go across.

On the top row of the spreadsheet (above) in the **A1** position, type in a heading entitled **Time**. In the **A2** position enter your event start time. Example: 6:00 PM.

Working your way down the A column break the event down to five-minute intervals by entering those times, working your way to the time that the event ends. Example: 6:05 PM, 6:10 PM, etc.

Your second column **B1** should be titled **Time Allotted**. In this column, next to the appropriate time row, you will place the amount of time you have allowed for the activity. Example: Opening & Welcoming Comments 3 Minutes.

Your third column **C1** should be labelled **Start Time** and the next one **D1, End Time.**

Your fifth column **E1** should be labelled **Activity**. Identify the activity in as few words as you can to describe the activity. Example: Opening

Comments. The activity description should be entered in the corresponding time row.

The sixth column **F1** will be labelled **Who?** As you fill out the spreadsheet, you will enter the name of the person who is most responsible for this particular activity. Example: 7:02 PM Welcoming Comments – Emcee.

I am a logistical thinker and I use the sixth column **G1**, labelled **Logistics** as a place to identify any logistics or concerns related to a specific activity. Example: Need to place certificates in the lectern, Move lectern out of the way for this speaker. Your comments should be entered into the box that corresponds with the specific activity.

I use the sixth column **H1** as a place to fit in any comments that don't necessarily fit into the Logistics Column.

This document is your working tool to organize your thoughts and all the event's activities.

Agendas often evolve over time rather than being created in one session. I would suggest you use the *Version* method of saving your files.

Every time I work on agenda, I save it with the current day's date. Example: ***Breakfast With Mayor Event v23-09-19***. If I worked on the file a few days later, I would save the file as ***Breakfast With Mayor Event v26-09-19***. This allows you to save your work incrementally so should you need to go back to a specific date you made a change, you can readily do so.

It is not unusual to experience the thought of "What in the world was I thinking when I changed...?" Having access to previous versions is helpful.

If you are sharing your spreadsheet with others, it is advisable to ensure you are all looking at the same version. It can be quite frustrating when discussing a specific line item, only to find you are working on different versions.

In addition, if you are sharing your spreadsheet and they may be making changes to it, it can be helpful if you upload the document to a cloud storage site such as Dropbox or Google Docs. That way a few people can have the same document open on their computer screen in front of them and discuss it while on a telephone conference call, or webinar/screen sharing program.

DOCUMENT TWO (PROGRAM AGENDA): FROM THE *DOCUMENT 1 Minute-by-Minute Timeline* you have created, copy the **Start Time** & **Activities** and paste them into a Word document (or whatever word processing program you have access to.) This will become your working Agenda or Program.

You will probably need to flesh it out with more details such as credentials for different individuals who will be speaking. This document in turn will become the official Agenda/Program for your event.

Event	
6:00	Registration Opens
6:45	Guests move to Hall
7:00	Opening & Welcoming Comments
7:03	Comments from Sponsor
7:08	Introduction of Keynote Speaker
7:10	Keynote speaker
8:00	Thank Keynote & present gift
8:02	Welcome to awards ceremony
8:04	Introduce Award Ceremony Sponsor
8:06	Awards Ceremony
8:56	Closing Remarks
9:00	Adjourn

HERE IS ANOTHER EXAMPLE [BELOW] OF A TIMELINE DERIVED FROM BOTH the *Minute-by-minute Timeline* and a *Program Agenda.* Note that colour has been added to the spreadsheet to help differentiate the activities on the agenda.

Also note coffee breaks and transition times have been factored in. If your guests have to move from one room to another, you need to factor in time for them to do so.

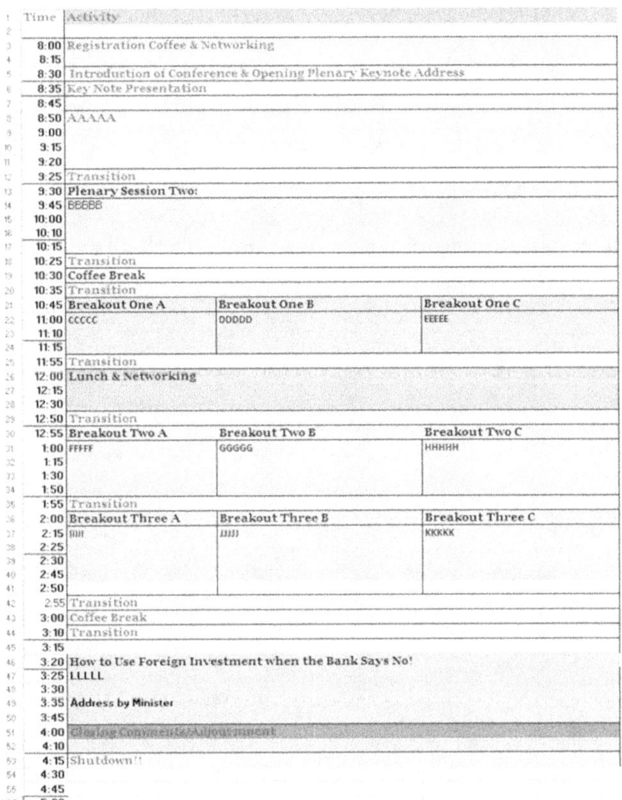

Time	Activity		
8:00	Registration Coffee & Networking		
8:15			
8:30	Introduction of Conference & Opening Plenary Keynote Address		
8:35	Key Note Presentation		
8:45			
8:50	AAAAA		
9:00			
9:15			
9:20			
9:25	Transition		
9:30	**Plenary Session Two:**		
9:45	BBBBB		
10:00			
10:10			
10:15			
10:25	Transition		
10:30	**Coffee Break**		
10:35	Transition		
10:45	**Breakout One A**	**Breakout One B**	**Breakout One C**
11:00	CCCCC	DDDDD	EEEEE
11:10			
11:15			
11:55	Transition		
12:00	**Lunch & Networking**		
12:15			
12:30			
12:50	Transition		
12:55	**Breakout Two A**	**Breakout Two B**	**Breakout Two C**
1:00	FFFFF	GGGGG	HHHHH
1:15			
1:30			
1:50			
1:55	Transition		
2:00	**Breakout Three A**	**Breakout Three B**	**Breakout Three C**
2:15	IIIII	JJJJJ	KKKKK
2:25			
2:30			
2:45			
2:50			
2:55	Transition		
3:00	Coffee Break		
3:10	Transition		
3:15			
3:20	**How to Use Foreign Investment when the Bank Says No!**		
3:25	LLLLL		
3:30			
3:35	**Address by Minister**		
3:45			
4:00	Closing Comments/Adjournment		
4:10			
4:15	Shutdown!!		
4:30			
4:45			
5:00			

DOCUMENT THREE (EMCEE NOTES): WHILE THE **MINUTE-MINUTE Time Line** document is a great way to get your thoughts organized, larger spreadsheets tend to be unwieldy when you print them.

Much the same as creating the agenda in **Document Two Program Agenda** above, I create a word document with the agenda copied into it. This becomes my minute-by-minute script for my role as the Emcee. I don't leave anything to chance.

I don't necessarily read it word for word out loud during the event but it is there to keep me organized should I need it. With so many small details, I usually do need it.

In my notes I identify the script I want to say in a bold font. I make use of point form notes to myself. "Remember to…" I will also phonetically spell out a speaker's name that may be problematic from a delivery perspective.

We will discuss using your *Emcee Notes* later in this book and two examples will be explored. **See Introductory Scripts.**

6. THINK LOGISTICALLY: WHAT ELSE DO YOU NEED TO PREPARE FOR?

You will have likely noticed by now I give a lot of importance to thinking logistically. In fact, I had to think logistically in writing this book, making sure I have provided you the reader with enough information so you can perform effectively as an Emcee, yet not too much to bog you down.

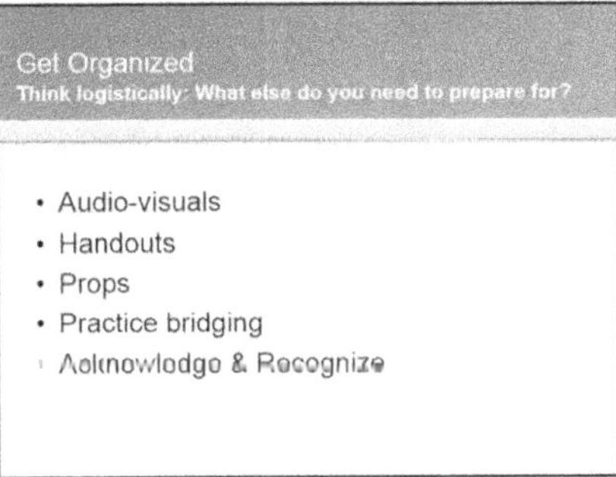

In this section we explore the additional Emcee roles of using audio-visuals, handouts, props, bridging, acknowledging specific individuals and providing recognition.

Audio-Visuals:

In these days of rapidly progressing technology, audiences have come to expect state-of -the-art audio-visual equipment being used, or at least as close as you can get to it.

Gone are the days of the overhead projector with its plastic overhead sheets and challenges to keep the content in focus and provide a smooth transition between overheads. However, there were a lot of them sold so don't be surprised if one shows up at an event you are emceeing.

Handouts:

Handouts may or may not be critical to your role as the Emcee. They could come in the form of an agenda or meeting program or perhaps have relevance to a featured speaker.

The rule of thumb is not to introduce a handout until it is needed. On the other hand, there is the belief that rules [of thumb] are meant to be broken. Rules... not thumbs!

With the rapid evolvement of the internet many event organizers are requiring their speakers to prepare their handouts in advance, allowing them to be uploaded to the internet and then downloaded by the event participants before they attend the event.

The advantage to the event organizers is they can offload the expense of printing massive amounts of copies on to the event participant. In turn, the event organizer would arrange to have a few copies available at the venue for those who hadn't downloaded or forgot their copies.

The advantage to the event participants is they have access to speaker sessions they may not be able to attend. You can't be in two places at once, but you can certainly have the speaker's notes for two sessions at the same time.

The advantage to the speaker is they have an additional source to promote their products or services.

Many speakers/presenters will take responsibility for the distribution of their handouts, especially in a breakout session. In a plenary session, i.e. a presentation to the whole group, somebody has to ensure the handouts are distributed in an expedient and non-disruptive manner.

While it can be argued this task lays in the hands of the speaker, I go with the attitude of not assuming anything. We talk about working with speakers a little later on and whether they have handouts or not is a logistical question that should be answered.

Agendas/programs should be distributed in advance. One method is to place a copy on each empty seat you expect someone to occupy. Another way is to provide the event attendee with their copy when they register or check-in for the event at a Registration desk or table.

For handouts required during a presentation it can be helpful, and less distracting, to arrange for people on each side of the room to pass them out. The number needed would depend on the size of the room.

We talk about agendas elsewhere and one of your major responsibilities as the Emcee is to draw your audience's attention to the items on the agenda. One of your challenges of course is to stay on time. There will be people in the audience watching the timeline.

Agendas:

We have mentioned agendas a few times so far. One of your duties as an Emcee is to make your audience aware of the program's agenda and your role in keeping the program moving forward on time. The agenda is your roadmap for your event. Your opening remarks during your actual event should make reference to the agenda.

Quite often an item on the agenda can change after it has been printed. You should advise your audience if there has been changes so they can make a note of the correction in their agendas. You can't be responsible if they don't make the changes on their copy but at least you have done your due diligence by informing them of the change.

Props:

As I understand it, the word *props* comes from the word *properties* and originated in the theatre. *Property Managers* assured that all the objects or properties that were needed to make a scene credible, were present.

From a speaking perspective i.e. speaking from a stage or a specific area, props can take on different meanings. Any object on the stage, except the speaker of course, can be considered a prop.

If you are of an age to remember them, many celebrities are known for their props. Bob Hope went on stage with a golf club. George Burns always had a big cigar. They became known for their props and their props served a purpose in their presentation.

Later we talk about working with speakers. One of the logistical questions to ask them is if they have a prop they want to placed somewhere in the speaking area, in advance, so they can easily bring attention to it when they want to.

Props can have a negative effect as well. Anything in the speaking area that takes away from the effectiveness of the speaker can be considered as being a negative prop. This may come in the form of chairs, tables, lecterns, microphones etc. that are placed inappropriately. You may need to intervene in advance if you see problems.

TRANSITIONS/BRIDGING:

Bridging between speakers or between items on an agenda is an art. When an Emcee does it smoothly the audience probably doesn't even notice. However, when it is done poorly, they certainly do.

Many Emcees make the mistake of trying to be funny, or as the saying goes 'stealing the speaker's thunder.' Your role is to ensure the speaker gets the attention they deserve.

Many Emcees create their bridging in advance and then deliver it as they would the lines of a script. The challenge in this is you need to deliver your lines in a manner that doesn't sound canned.

I tend to create my bridging on the fly. While the speaker is delivering their content, I am multi-tasking. I am preparing for the next function I need to undertake. At the same time, I am listening for *"gems"* I can comment on in my bridging. I try to be entertaining in my comments but not at the expense of the speaker or to make me look better.

It can be helpful when researching about the upcoming event that you dig to find humorous trivia about the participating audience (especially the leaders!) and have these tidbits readily available to use throughout the meeting. You may not be able to fit any or all of them in but it could really make a difference in your performance if you have the opportunity to do so.

OUTRODUCTIONS:

This is a made-up word I have been hearing lately and is related to the comments the speaker would like you to say, after their presentation. Similar to bridging, where you acknowledge the speaker's content and presentation, it also serves the purpose of drawing attention to an area the speaker wants attention drawn to. If they have this in mind, they will advise you in advance.

It could be a matter of mentioning a special offer or a free giveaway the speaker offered in their presentation. As the Emcee you have to ensure you allow enough time for this extra. The minutes have a way of adding up.

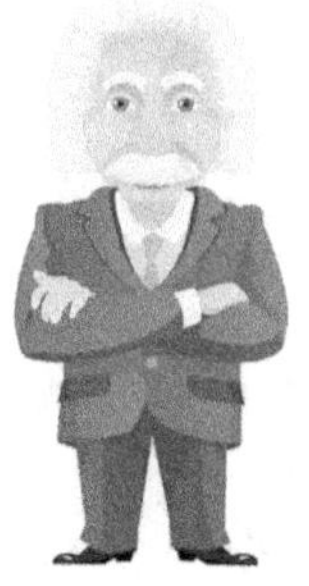

ON TRANSITIONS:

- If the topic is emotional, give it time to sink in.
- Never deliver abrupt transitions... keep it smooth.
- Get the audience into neutral before moving on.
- Have quick short stories or quotes available for filler. Use as needed. (they should have some relevance to the topic)
- Refer back to previous speakers when introducing the next speaker.
- Help to weave a thread so it's one continuous event rather than just separate speeches.

On Acknowledging & Recognizing:

Depending upon the nature of the event, acknowledging and recognizing specific individuals may be as important as the content of the event itself.

In a formal event it may be necessary to address the organization's VIPs (Very Important People) or visiting dignitaries in your opening comments. I would recommend researching the correct or expected titles as part of your presentation. There are too many titles to discuss here.

A Mayor would likely be introduced as "Her/His Worship, Mayor of...." Perhaps a Member of Parliament as "The Honourable Member from Kicking Horse Pass..."

Another Rule of Thumb comes to play in that protocol dictates that the person with the higher standing, would be introduced first.

From the Toastmaster's world of protocol we would often hear "Madame District Governor, District Executive, fellow Toastmasters and honoured guests." While it does follow a strict format, it doesn't mean to say that our guests are at the bottom of the pile.

Recognition also comes in the form of presenting awards to individuals during the program. We discuss that a little later in the book.

On Applause:

As the Emcee you are the cheerleader for the event. Your audience will look to you for direction on how they should respond. You need to lead the applause right after you introduce a speaker, inviting them up to speak and after they have completed their presentation.

This is your opportunity to be creative. Consider the traditional "Let's give a round of applause for..." If you really think about it... applause is not always round nor does it always come in rounds, so with a little creativity I am certain you can think of ways to welcome someone to the stage rather than the clichés we often hear.

Instead, consider "Help me welcome to the lectern...", "Please show your appreciation for...", "Let's give a warm welcome to...", "Please join me in welcoming...", "By your applause, let's show our gratitude...", "How about a nice hand for...."

ON HECKLERS:

- Closer is better if you have control of the mic. Make your way to the heckler, as you're talking to the audience, and put your hand on their shoulder. "By the way sir, who are you or what do you do?"
- Acknowledge the heckler and then move on. Praise them... the unsung heroes.

7. WHAT TO WEAR?

The rule of thumb is to dress one level above how your audience will be dressing. This is probably one area that separates the amateur Emcees from the professionals.

There are several factors that come into play e.g. time of the year, temperature hot/cold, the culture of the organization and the nature of the event.

Where your audience will be expected to be dressed in "business casual" it would be appropriate for men to dress in a suit or sports jacket with matching dress pants.

For women, hmmm… good question. I haven't got my head wrapped around women's fashion. I have seen professional women emcee an event attired in a ball gown and I have wondered if it was appropriate for the event. What seems to work is a business casual pant suit.

Formal events, often called "black tie" would indicate you as the Emcee should wear a tuxedo. I have been to black tie events, and I have seen men that didn't quite understand the concept of formal. To them it seemed to mean they wear their cleanest blue jeans and a string bow tie.

You can't control what other people wear but *you* can raise the bar by dressing professionally. Your image, or how people see you, will go a long way in marketing your professional image.

Here's some sage advice I learned the hard way. If you go into the restroom to use the facilities, ensure you do your fly up when you return.

I was on stage for a good hour or so, and was sitting on the side while a speech contestant was presenting. I looked down and noticed my fly was undone. I was mortified. As I was still in full view and unable to zip up, I had to carry on up the lectern and carry on as if nothing was wrong. Once behind the lectern, I zipped up. Fortunately, I was wearing black pants with black underwear and likely only I noticed the wardrobe malfunction.

8. WORKING WITH SPEAKERS

Will there be speakers at your event?

As the Emcee it will be your role to *facilitate* the Speaker's portion of the agenda. I use the term *facilitate* because you have several duties that will take place before the event, while the speaker is presenting and after the speaker has completed their delivery.

The following content explores the art of introducing a speaker. After that we will explore the Emcee's facilitation roles.

LET ME INTRODUCE... THE ART OF INTRODUCING A SPEAKER:
Practical Tips & Techniques

Have you ever heard this said "Our next speaker needs no introduction..." Well, if that's true Mister/Madam Emcee, then why do we need you?

As a *Master* of Ceremonies your role is to build excitement about each and every speaker or presenter on your agenda.

While developing and honing my speaking skills at countless Toastmasters meetings and introducing hundreds of speakers and their speeches over the years, I have developed an appreciation for the value of an effective introduction.

Whether you are introducing a speaker/presenter, presenting an award or introducing a person who will be taking on a role in the program, a professionally written and delivered introduction can exponentially increase the effectiveness of the person you are introducing.

As the Master of Ceremonies you are the warm-up act! Your role is to build excitement so your audience can't wait to hear what the person you are introducing has to say.

Here are some tips & techniques to ensure your next speaker introductions are delivered professionally.

Preparation is the key to success. If you are introducing a professional or very experienced speaker, they may provide you with a script in advance that they want you to deliver word for word... nothing more, nothing less.

They will also likely provide you with details or instructions on how to deliver the introduction. You may be told to read it quickly with an increasing tempo or perhaps slow and whimsical.

It all depends on what they are trying to achieve in their presentation.

If you can memorize some of it without having to read your notes word for word, all the better.

As an Emcee I have often met the speaker just moments before they go on stage with them passing me their introduction and only having a quick view of what I will be reading.

If you can contact your speaker in advance to work out the details of their introduction, do so.

But what about the nonprofessional speaker who when asked for an introduction of their presentation replies with "Oh you know me. Just make something up!" What will you do then?

I would muster up my creative writing skills and craft an award-winning introduction. Okay, the awards haven't been coming too quickly yet, if not at all!

Using the six questions of who, what, why, when, where and how that every story requires, you would start by gathering answers to each of those vital questions.

This information gathering leads to the next step of the process I call creating *promotional copy*. That is a term borrowed from the direct marketing industry to promote and sell products or services.

Selling the speaker to the audience

The most important factor we have to address from the audience's perspective is "what's in it for me?" Those that are awake and not texting on their smart phones that is.

Each audience member is asking the same questions: "Why should I listen to this person?" "Where is their credibility?" "What promises are they making me?"

I am sure it would be quite easy to build a long list of thoughts that go through an audience member's minds while awaiting an upcoming speaker. "I hope they don't go on and on... I have to go to the bathroom!"

If the person I am introducing is speaking on a topic chosen for them in advance and they have been chosen to speak because they have expertise on the subject, I would build that fact into my introduction.

I would mention any academic achievements or honorary awards they have been presented if it adds to their credibility. I would do my best to highlight their accomplishments and promote what sage wisdom they will likely have to share with us.

Your introduction serves as the warm up act in helping your speaker to a strong start.

For some speakers you may need to impose a limit to the amount you say about them. I am reminded of a workshop I attended where the introducer of the presenter advised us that when she contacted the speaker who was a psychologist, for biographical information to do the introduction, she was provided with a 32 page fax of the doctor's accomplishments. I was impressed until the point I realized she was intending to read every word on every page of all 32 pages!

Sometimes as an Emcee you will encounter a speaker that is lacklustre, some may call them *"plain vanilla."* That probably begs the question "why are they speaking if that is true?"

Your challenge as a promotional copy writer is to work with them and dig a little to find those personal details that will "sell" the speaker.

Your digging might even reveal an astounding fact your speaker doesn't boast about, that while not directly related to the topic at hand, has great relevance.

Have you ever wondered how athletes or celebrities become motivational speakers? Their stardom enables them to springboard into other topics that brings their credibility with them. Your job is to find that hidden nugget and shine it — but review it with the speaker before presenting live.

It can be embarrassing for the speaker to hear an introduction that wasn't true, the whole truth and nothing but the truth. Other's, may be embarrassed to have their accomplishments revealed publicly.

Now as for introducing a featured speaker who has a prepared speech or presentation, the process is essentially the same with the addition of promotional copy to build excitement about the topic as well as the speaker. Why is this topic important or of value to the audience? Why this particular speaker? Why now?

You require the assistance of your speaker in crafting this promo.

What information does your speaker want you to impart upon the audience? Does the speaker want the audience all fired up or in a thoughtful mood? Does your audience need to be focused on something before the speaker starts?

Asking rhetorical questions of the audience can be beneficial. "Who among us believes..." "Have you ever found yourself... our speaker has! And they can't wait to tell you how they..."

Your introduction should be crafted as any other speech. It should include an opening, body and conclusion. The slight difference in telling a story is you are building the excitement as part of the speaker's story and it is up to them to finish it.

Pitfalls to avoid:

1. You don't want to create a promotional introduction that might embarrass the speaker.

2. Avoid making statements the speaker couldn't possibly live up to. Example: "You are going to absolutely love this speaker. He is the funniest man alive. He makes Robin Williams look like Richard Nixon!" If it is true... go for it! If not... don't use it.

3. Do not steal the speaker's thunder! Perhaps you have heard the speaker's presentation before. Mentioning the content or paraphrasing their lines can take away the impact of the material when the speaker is presenting it. I would suggest confirming with the speaker that your introduction adds to their presentation and not take away from it. I have experienced far too many occasions where I have been asked to give a few words on a subject with short notice only to find that the introducer has said almost word for word what I was about to deliver.

4. Don't wing it. *Practice, practice, practice!* Despite how the cliché goes, practice does not make perfect. Practice with constructive feedback and acting upon the suggestions, leads

to excellence. Rehearse your introductions out loud and have a partner provide you with feedback as to what worked, what didn't and what you could do to improve your presentation. Toastmasters clubs are excellent places to practice these skills and receive constructive feedback.

AN IMPORTANT TIP NOT MENTIONED IN THE ABOVE ARTICLE IS TO ENSURE you pronounce your speaker's name correctly. Dale Carnegie in his classic **'How to Win Friends and Influence People'** says "Remember that a person's name is to that person the sweetest and most important sound in any language." What you see in writing may not be the way that they pronounce it. Ask the speaker to pronounce it phonetically.

EXAMPLE ONE: EMCEE INTRODUCTORY SCRIPT

Here is an example of a script I used to welcome guests to an event and introduce the two featured speakers. You will notice I used **Bold** and *Italics* on many of the words or phrases. I did this to remind me to put emphasis on these highlighted words to draw extra attention to them. I haven't done it here but I also write my notes with 14 or 16 font size so that I am better able to read them at the lectern.

Good evening everyone and welcome to the July Townhall of the **Okanagan Valley Entrepreneurs Society (OVES)**. I'm Rae Stonehouse and I'm the Chairman of the Board for OVES as well as being your **Moderator** for this evening.

Our theme this evening **Midsummer Social Media Marketing Mania: What's Hot, What's Not & What's Plain Rot!**

Well we could probably answer the question of "**What's hot?**" by saying the "Okanagan is" but you already know that. This evening we are going to take an in depth look at **social media** and figure out *why, how and what* an already busy entrepreneur should be doing.

I would like to remind everyone that our Townhalls are sponsored by the **Kelowna Scotiabank** which has made these events possible over the past few years.

We have two panellists this evening who are going to share their *skills, experience and sage advice* with us.

LET'S MEET THEM.

XXXXXXXXXX:

I FIRST MET **XXXXXXXXXX** EARLIER THIS YEAR AT A LOCAL **J**UNIOR **Chamber International** monthly meeting where I was a guest speaker and she was a member. Then I met her at a networking breakfast for the **Okanagan Business Referral Group.** One of her taglines is *"Life is about being social... and so is business."* It looks to me that she is *walking her talk.*

AS THE OWNER OF **AAAAAA, XXXXXXXXXX** HELPS BUSINESSES navigate the social landscape.

SHE HAS SPENT 20 YEARS IN SALES, MARKETING, AND MANAGEMENT IN multinational companies such as Hewlett Packard, Sysco Food Services and Yum Brands... these are in the retail, restaurant, and technology fields. This allows her to bring a wealth of additional MARKETING knowledge to help guide a business's SOCIAL MEDIA

MARKETING STRATEGY. And that is what we are really here to talk about this evening.

As the owner of **AAAAAA** she works with small business owners, consultants, and entrepreneurs to help them use social media to connect to their existing and potential clients. She and her company specializes in social media management, strategizing, consulting, training & coaching.

Please welcome **XXXXXXXXX.**

Our second panellist specializes in *Social Media and Online Marketing.* She is a returning panellist having shared her experience with on-line marketing on a *previous* Townhall.

As the owner of **BBBBBB, ZZZZZZZZ** brings over twenty years of experience to the business.

She has owned a Website Development & Print Design Firm prior to having children.

While her kids were little, she returned to the corporate world where she polished her existing skills and learned a few new tricks.

Her children are now at an age where she can revive her entrepreneurial spirit and she says that she couldn't be more excited!

Over the past few months she has also taken on *a Director position with OVES* and we are grateful for her sharing her expertise with us.

PLEASE WELCOME **ZZZZZZZZ.**

SO LET'S GET STARTED. ARE THERE ANY FIRST TIMERS HERE THIS evening? *Welcome.* The idea behind our Townhalls is that we have our sage experts at the front of the room and we have you the audience who have more than likely come with some specific questions.

This will be an *interactive* discussion not a lecture so if you have a question that is related to our topic at the time, please ask it. We will also be taking a networking break at 8:15 to 8:30, then finishing by 9 pm.

Our topic once again is **Midsummer Social Media Marketing Mania: What's Hot, What's Not & What's Plain Rot!**

~

EXAMPLE TWO: EMCEE NOTES

Here are the Emcee notes from a daylong event I organized and served as the Emcee. Note the **MC Notes** helped remind me of important tasks I needed to do with each speaker. Once again, I use **Bold** & *Italics* to draw my attention to words I needed to accentuate.

8:30 CALL TO ORDER... OPENING COMMENTS

Good morning everyone and welcome to the Okanagan Valley Entrepreneurs Society *OVES* as I call it, *Finding Strength Within the Forest Conference.* I'm Rae Stonehouse, I'm Chairman of the Board of Directors for OVES and I will be serving as your emcee for today. My entrepreneurial adventure is called *Mr. Emcee.* Guess what I do?

I was telling my wife recently that a definition of an entrepreneur is having the freedom to work *any 24 hours a day*, **every day**, that you choose. I have certainly found that out working day in day out over the past month on this conference. I would expect that I have either e-mailed each one of you numerous times or spoken to you on the phone.

If you read our program for the day, you will that this is also being billed as the *First ever Annual Entrepreneurial Conference.* I'm already thinking ahead to the *tenth* annual conference. It's the *second through eighth one* that have me pulling my hair out. And I can't afford to that much more. People are going to start calling me XXXXXX if I lose anymore.

Conferences such as this wouldn't be possible without the help of our sponsors. I would like to thank our title sponsor of *MacKay Accountants* as well as *Accelerate Okanagan and the Province of BC Ministry of Jobs, Tourism and Skills Training* for their support.

Last evening I was kidding XXXXX one of our Exhibitors from Province of BC Ministry of Jobs, Tourism and Skills Training that answering the phone at their office must be interesting. You would hope there was still somebody on the other end of the line when you finished saying who you were.

We have a tight agenda today and my job is to keep us to time. Wish me luck!

8:45–9:30

Our first speaker this morning has the challenge of starting our entrepreneurial conference off to a strong start. He completed his commercial pilot's license in 1967 and has accumulated over 17,000 hours of flying time. I got curious about that number and worked it out that he has spent over two years in the air.

When not in the air he moved to the Okanagan Valley in 1968 and started Kelowna Flightcraft shortly after in 1970.

The company initially performed only maintenance inspection checks. But over the years this has expanded to courier and charter services, aircraft maintenance, and is now one of the largest Maintenance Repair Operations in Canada.

KFL is now the third largest airline company in Canada, by fleet size, and is one of the oldest privately owned aviation companies in Canada today.

The KFL Group of Companies is a success story, which has now grown to over 1000 employees and numerous operations across Canada. These operate out of 2 main bases in Kelowna and Hamilton, as well as 8 satellite bases that stretch across Canada from Vancouver, B.C. to St. John's Newfound Land.

If by chance, you haven't heard of Kelowna Flight craft before perhaps you have seen them in action. If you wondered about some of the lights that you see flying across our night skies, those that aren't aliens or space junk of course, they are probably KFL airplanes. They are the exclusive air cargo carrier for Purolator Courier (PCL) and Canada Post and have been flying the night sky across Canada providing the capability of moving approximately a million pounds of freight nightly, to every major city in Canada.

Please welcome XXXXX.

MC Note: Don't forget Chocolate gift. "As a small token of our appreciation I would like to present you with this gift." Another round of applause for Barry.

And now we are going to divert from our agenda for a couple moments. We have an award presentation to a deserving individual and we would to share it with you.

I would like to invite the *Honourable XXXXX* for Kelowna Lake Country to present the award. XXXXX

. . .

Diamond Jubilee Medal (background info to use if Presenter doesn't elaborate)

Queen Elizabeth II Diamond Jubilee Medal

A new commemorative medal was created to mark the 2012 celebrations of the 60th anniversary of Her Majesty Queen Elizabeth II's accession to the Throne as Queen of Canada. The Queen Elizabeth II Diamond Jubilee Medal is a tangible way for Canada to honour Her Majesty for her service to this country. At the same time, it serves to honour significant contributions and achievements by Canadians.

During the year of celebrations, 60,000 deserving Canadians will be recognized. Recipient was nominated by the Canadian Youth Business Foundation.

Offer congrats to recipient

9:30-10:15 *Fail to plan* and you *plan to fail*. An often heard *entrepreneurial cliché.* We know you *go into a business* with the idea you are *going to succeed.* You try to cover all your bases so failure isn't an option. *But what if you really do succeed?* Have you allowed for that in your business plan? Have you planned for investors to invest in your business? This session will give us tips on how to interest an investor.

This presentation is a tag team one if you will. I don't know if they will slap each other like you in the wrestling matches on TV, but you never know.

XXXXX is a Professor at the Okanagan School of Business, Okanagan College and is a professional advisor to business.

YYYYY is an entrepreneur. On October 26th, 2010 as the owner and operator of Enquiro, they began operating as Mediative, A Yellow Pages Group Company.

Mediative is one of North America's largest integrated digital marketing companies.

Their Presentation... **The Incomparable Business Plan – Creating Expectations.** Please welcome *XXXXX and YYYYY.*

MC Note: Don't forget Chocolate gift! "As a small token of our appreciation I would like to present you with this gift"

Thanks again XXXXX and YYYYY

10:15-10:30 Break Please be back in your seats by *about 10:27.* We have a tight schedule today and I'm going to do my best to keep to it. If you are late coming in please be quiet in consideration of our speakers. If not I may have you stand in a corner. Let's take a break. Coffee and refreshments are in the display room and don't forget to talk to *someone* you don't know yet!

10:30-11:15 This next session will focus on entrepreneurial ideas and opportunities. If I had a dollar for every time I have heard from an entrepreneur or entrepreneur wannabee *"You know I've got this idea rattling around my head that's going to make a lot of money..."* Well if I did get a dollar each time, I guess I would be a wealthy entrepreneur and I could do something about all the *money-making ideas that rattle around in my head.*

Our next speaker seems to have done *something* about those ideas she has had. She began holding and managing single family properties in 1998 at the age of 23. I leave you to do the math to figure out how old she is now.

In 2001 as the *founder and currently the CEO* of the Kelowna-based Troika Group of Companies, which includes construction and development and a millwork manufacturing company, together employing 50 people.

Troika has active projects with over 2500 units in three provinces.

She was ranked in *BC Home Magazines 2012 Top 20 Most Influential*

Industry Leaders, won *2008 Business Excellence Award recipient for the Young Entrepreneur of the Year*, achieved the Business in Vancouver's Top 40 Under 40 award in 2009 as well as all of her projects achieving Tommie recognition.

In *2007* she was a finalist for the Sarah Donalda Treadgold Memorial Award for Woman of the Year in Kelowna and Kelowna's Business Excellence Award.

When not CEOing and winning recognition awards, she is President of the Urban Development Institute (Okanagan), Chairman of the Economic Development Commission, serves on the Downtown Kelowna Association and on the Breakfast Clubs of Canada National Board.

I think that she likely has more than a few money making ideas bouncing around in her head. Her presentation... **Being Prepared... Ideas vs Opportunities/ Innovation & Creativity.**

Please welcome XXXXX.

MC Note: Don't forget Chocolate gift! "As a small token of our appreciation I would like to present you with this gift"

Thanks again XXXXX.

11:15–12:00

Product development and *promotion* usually involve substantial costs in time, energy and money which would be wasted unless *venture ideas and innovations* are fully protected against poachers and imitators. Wow, that's a pretty ominous statement!

Several legal regimes exist for the protection of ideas and innovation. Every entrepreneur should know how to use them in their venture planning.

We might need a lawyer to explain that sentence. *Actually our next speaker is a lawyer*. In fact, he is an *intellectual property lawyer*, a registered Trade Mark agent and a registered Canadian and US patent agent. He has been advising his clients in copyright protection, intellectual property matters, Intellectual property licensing and protection for *over 20 years in both Canada and the USA.*

His company is called Horsepower Intellectual Law and his topic is Who Owns the Idea/Financing Innovation.

Please welcome **XXXXX.**

MC Note: Don't forget Chocolate gift! "As a small token of our appreciation I would like to present you with this gift"

Thanks again XXXXX.

12:00 lunch: It is set up in the other room as a buffet. You can either stay in there to socialize or bring your meal back to this room. We start up again at 12:45.

12:45-1:30

We have heard this morning that we *can, and must, reduce uncertainty, mitigate risk and eliminate some of the fear factor* through thorough *preparation* and *understanding* of the needs and objectives of both the investor and the innovator.

Adventure means *risk, excitement and boldness.* Successful venture capital investing requires the cooperation of both investors and **entrepreneurs** who boldly embrace and manage risk.

OUR NEXT SPEAKER HAS LED *SIX* SUCCESSFUL TECHNOLOGY COMPANIES, including OmniGlobe which he grew from zero revenue to near $25 million over a 5-year period before its sale, Lynx Mobility, a National cellular carrier with sites across Northern Canada and

TSA, a UK telecommunications outsourcer.

Over a *22 year career* he has raised near 35 million dollars of funding and exited twice.

He has turned around *three companies*, blown *two companies up* and has *three* projects still in progress.

His success as a serial entrepreneur has led to his distinction as an Ernest & Young Entrepreneur of Year winner as well as being named a Deloitte Fast 50 top 10 CEO.

He holds a PhD in *Electronic Engineering*, *Executive MBAs* from Columbia Business School and London Business School and is a graduate of the prestigious 1 year Entrepreneurship Development Program from MIT.

Recently, he turned VeriCorder around, a local technology company, that he transformed from a NEGATIVE 500k EBITDA company to a POSITIVE 70k EBITDA company in just over 8 months. In his current *'gig'*, he is the CEO of a media play, Visland Media and the CEO of a mobile Communications startup, Backcountry Mobile.

His presentation is *Taking the Adventure out of Venture Capital*. Please welcome *XXXXX*.

MC Note: Don't forget Chocolate gift! "As a small token of our appreciation I would like to present you with this gift"

1:45–2:30

Every business venture may be carried on through any one of a number of structures.

Choosing the right structure for your venture involves considering a wide range of issues.

Making the right decisions also involves issues like personal liability, control of ownership, financing & taxation. *Yes, ladies & gentlemen…* we need a lawyer to share their experience with all of those factors.

She is an *Associate* at Doak Shireff LLP Lawyers and her practice encompasses corporate commercial law, real estate law, employment law, strata property law and wills and estates.

Her objective is to obtain cost-effective results and find *creative and durable solutions* to *difficult* problems for her clients.

She received a Bachelor of Commerce degree from the University of Alberta in 1998, and a Masters in Business Administration, with a focus on *Marketing*, from Simon Fraser University in 1999.

She returned to the University of Alberta to obtain her Bachelor of Laws in 2007 and shortly thereafter she returned home to the Okanagan, and was called to the British Columbia bar in February 2009.

She brings a wide range of experience from her many years of *entrepreneurial ventures,* including new business creation and development, public relations, investor relations, marketing communications and real estate development. This experience enables her to provide her business clients, from small to large, with valuable insight and guidance in a variety of corporate and commercial matters.

Her presentation today *Your Entrepreneurial Venture and the Law*. Please welcome *XXXXX*.

MC NOTE: DON'T FORGET CHOCOLATE GIFT! "AS A SMALL TOKEN OF our appreciation I would like to present you with this gift"

2:40-3:20

As the *Canadian economy* restructures and *business and industry* strive to maintain competitiveness within our nation and globally, the entrepreneurial spirit and drive will help propel Canada forward into the next century.

This presentation will explore how financial institutions support the emerging strength of the entrepreneurial world. Additionally, a look at business conditions for Canadian **entrepreneurs** compared to those of the U.S.A.

Our next presentation is another tag team one. *XXXXX* is a 21 year veteran of the Pacific Northwest financial community, having spent the last *17 years* with Roynat Capital, one of the largest Merchant Banks in North America with $3 billion in assets.

His current role with Roynat is directing their Pacific Northwest

operations which include a *$200 Million investment portfolio* of mid-market

manufacturing/service and distribution companies with loans and investments in

the $1-$20MM range.

In his career with Roynat, he has been involved as a provider of Senior Term, Subordinated Debt and Equity, in numerous share-holder transactions including management buyouts, partner buyouts, equity recaps and acquisitions of various sizes and industries in Washington State and British Columbia.

He is joined by *YYYYY*. When I was writing my introductions late last evening, I found that *YYYYY* hadn't sent her Bio to me. Her words "I'll send it as soon as possible" I guess that means in banker's language... *"After the event."*

I like making stuff up. Let's give it a try.

She is the *Branch Manager* at Kelowna Main Branch & Commercial Banking Centre. I've known her vicariously over the past few years and more so over the past year as she and Kelowna Scotiabank have been sponsors for our OVES monthly Townhalls over the past several years.

Scotiabank also sponsors CBC Dragons Den & the Big Decision. They *seem to have* caught on. I'm waiting for my call to lead the Okanagan Entrepreneurs Reality Show. Perhaps I should speak to some of our guests on what kind of benefits package I should ask for. She is often observed saying "You are richer than you think!"

Their presentation is entitled *Emerging Strength in Entrepreneurial Venturing.*

Please welcome YYYYY and XXXXX.

MC Note: Don't forget Chocolate gift X2!! . "As a small token of our appreciation I would like to present you with this gift."

3:30–4:15

Our next session is a panel discussion with three real live entrepreneurs! Our Moderator is also a real entrepreneur. She is a **PASSION IGNITER** inspiring women and youth to REACH THEIR GOALS and FLOURISH at the same time. Her down-to-earth style is refreshing. Her messages are *clear, practical and transformational.* An expert on self-image, she teaches how everything in life comes down to the relationship we have with ourselves.

In addition to being a speaker, she is a radio broadcaster and business leader. She knows first-hand the *hardships and privileges* of *entrepreneurialism* and what it takes to ignite and maintain an attitude of success. And she is going to introduce her panel.

Please welcome *XXXXX.*

MC Note: Don't forget Chocolate gift X3!! . "As a small token of our appreciation I would like to present you with this gift."

4:15–5:00 PM

What is an *entrepreneur*? *Where* do they come from? *What value* are they to society?

I have often those very questions myself.

Our final speaker is the Manager of the Kelowna Business Centre for the Business Development Bank of Canada (BDC).

She brings a *wealth of experience* in working with businesses at all stages of development, with a passion for helping **entrepreneurs** grow their business and become more competitive.

Her background spans over *30 years*, working in the securities and investment field, term financing and subordinate and mezzanine financing.

She presently leads a team of account managers who are focused on promoting entrepreneurship within the Okanagan Valley, with a special consideration for the needs of small and medium-sized enterprises.

Her presentation will *sum up the discussions of our Conference and its focus*. She probably has the most challenging presentation in that she has had to listen to what everybody has said, condense it down even further.

Maintaining the Entrepreneurial Spirit... *XXXXX*

MC Note: Don't forget Chocolate gift Xɪ!! . "As a small token of our appreciation I would like to present you with this gift."

9. EMCEEING IN ACTION

At the risk of blatant self-promotion, which I don't have a problem with as it is the subject of one of my upcoming publications, please check out these videos that illustrate emceeing in action.

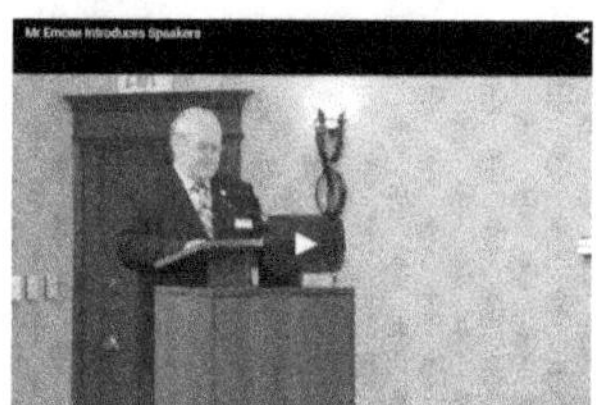

Video One: Mr. Emcee aka Rae Stonehouse demonstrating introducing speakers at the OVES Unleashing Ideas Conference November 2013 in Kelowna. https://www.youtube.com/watch?v=koneX89H-WQ

VIDEO TWO: RAE STONEHOUSE AKA MR. EMCEE DEMONSTRATES master of ceremonies opening comments at the Unleashing Ideas Conference hosted by the Okanagan Valley Entrepreneurs Society in Kelowna, B.C. in November 2013. Here is the link to the on-line video https://www.youtube.com/watch?v=3TBqeqXoQ4E

10. SPEAKER LOGISTICS

Thinking logistically continues to be a common thread through this book. In this chapter we look closer at what is involved in working with a speaker.

This is one of the roles you have as an Emcee. As a facilitator, it is your role to ensure the speakers have a higher chance of being successful. You can't guarantee their success... they have to do it themselves.

We previously discussed introducing a speaker effectively, however there are more logistics we need to consider that may not have addressed.

- What is the title of their presentation?
- How long will they be speaking?
- Where will they be speaking from?
- Will they be using a fixed mic i.e. attached to a lectern/podium, or will they be using a portable hand-held mic or perhaps a wireless lapel mic?
- Does the speaker have handouts? If so, how will they be distributed and by who(m)?
- Does the speaker plan to use props?

- If so, will they bring the props with them when they approach the speaking area or should they be in place when they arrive?
- Do you have the speaker's introduction ready?
- If the speaker is speaking on a stage or designated area, will there be enough lighting on them so that they can be seen by the audience?
- Do they have an outroduction that they would like you to present?

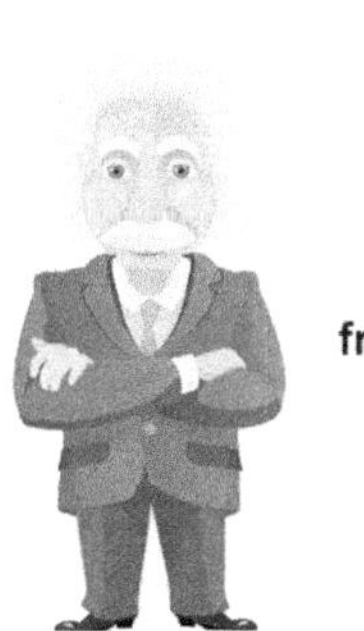

- Coach the speakers on the importance of speaking within their allotted time.
- Do not stay on the platform when a keynote speaker speaks. Have a place to go off stage, hopefully out of the limelight when a speaker is presenting. This area becomes your anchor. When off the stage, sit down.
- However, it is okay to stand to the side of someone who is performing a minor role.
- An Emcee is a nurturer or an enabler.
- Being an Emcee is an honour not a burden.
- You want to be helpful but not intrusive. "How can I be of service?"

More Tips from the Pros:

- Enthusiasm will carry you through a long event -- keep YOUR energy up so the audience stays with you.
- Pacing is important to meet that main objective -- time your stories or energizers and modify accordingly.
- Obvious, but needs to be said: stay gracious, happy and flexible.
- It's helpful if you have some material planned in case of a no-show or some presenters that speak significantly less than the time expected.

11. AND THE WINNER IS... THE ART OF PRESENTING AWARDS: PRACTICAL TIPS & TECHNIQUES

While participating in sports as a young person growing up I was a member of several teams that were presented with awards of recognition but was never the recipient of an individual award.

Awards were based on proficiency and results. I displayed neither. Elementary and secondary school weren't any different. Apparently there wasn't an annual award presented for showing up.

This left me unprepared for my first experience as a presenter of an award of recognition. I was serving as the Student Council President in my second year of training as a nurse in a community college when I was called upon to present a silver gavel to the President of the college as a token of appreciation for his many years of service.

When it was my turn to speak and make the presentation... the cameras recording the moment for prosperity... I panicked and uttered the words "I'm so scared up here!"

Things got a little black as I recall. I'm pretty sure I remained standing during the ordeal and I'm not sure how the President ever got his gavel.

In a strange twist of fate, the President took his own life a few short weeks later. I don't think my mishandling of the ceremony had had anything to do with it, or so my therapist convinced me.

Award presentation ceremonies aren't life and death situations nor will they be effective without advance preparation and your self-confidence to put on a good show. Think showmanship. Think about some award presentation ceremonies you have seen in the past as to what worked and what didn't.

I believe two of the biggest mistakes amateur or inexperienced Emcees make are that they are unprepared and/or make the ceremony about themselves rather than the award recipient.

Humour and jokes can be a powerful tool when used effectively but when they are used to make *you* the star of the show, they are not.

It's not about you! Your job is to entertain and inform your audience and convince them the award you are presenting at that moment and the person receiving the award are of great importance.

Being an effective Emcee is an art. Like a giant iceberg with much of its bulk hidden beneath the waters, much of what happens in an award presentation ceremony is done behind the scenes before the spotlight shines on you.

Here are some steps to take to ensure your next award presentation is handled professionally.

Logistics: (things that you need to know in advance)

- Do the nominees know in advance if they have won a specific award or just their nomination?
- Does the agenda allow time for the winners to deliver an acceptance speech? If so, how long are they allowed?
- If there are multiple awards to be presented, do you know the total time allotted in the agenda?
- What are the sizes of the awards? Will they be placed on a

nearby table or perhaps hidden within the lectern/podium? Will you be able to lift them or will you require an assistant?

Research questions:

- What is the award being presented for?
- Does the award/trophy have a name?
- What were the criteria for winning the award?
- Are there any notable past winners that should be mentioned?
- What did the recipient of the award do to win the award? Examples: specific accomplishments or achievements.
- How was the winner chosen and perhaps from how many if the number is known?
- Does the winner get to keep the award forever or for a period of time?
- Is there a sponsor for the particular award? Are you expected to do a promotional plug for them as well or will they be expected to speak?

Preparation: Creating your script

You should incorporate the answers to your research questions into your speaker's notes. Answer the questions of who, what, why, when, where and how. Your role is to create excitement about the award being presented even if it is an award that in your mind is a big whoop-dee-doo. (i.e. not really very important at all.)

Your notes should be written for the spoken word, not the written. Short sentences. Simple words. Lots of adjectives. They should be appropriate ones though and not flowery.

You should be enthusiastic and motivational in your presentation, yet at the same time, sincere. You can read your notes at the time of the presentation if you really need to control your nervousness however, you will seem to be more polished and professional if you have committed much of your content to memory and only refer to your notes for specific details you want to ensure are delivered correctly.

Presenting the Award:

Its show time! All eyes are on you. It's time to raise some excitement. It's time to make a special person feel like they are the most important person in the world, at least for the next few moments. You have your script. If it is a trophy, a plaque or an object of some kind, this would be a good time to show it to the audience.

Start by introducing the background of the award, why it is so important and provide examples of what the winner has done to achieve the award. By now, if the nominees for the award haven't been told in advance they have won, they will likely recognize their achievements being broadcasted.

Now is time to announce the winner. Your voice can be an effective tool by increasing your speaking speed, your pitch and your volume as you build your audience into a frenzy of anticipation. Well, maybe in your mind! Your role at this point is to act as a cheerleader and lead the applause as you announce the winner and invite them up to you to receive their award.

If you have a co-presenter, it would be prudent to give a brief intro of them before you started your delivery. They might be the sponsor of the award. Having a previous winner of the award pass it on to the next winner can be quite exciting.

If you are the sole presenter of the award, step away from the lectern/podium to allow room to present the award and shake the recipient's hand. Think photo op. Hopefully, you have remembered to dress in your finest.

While shaking the winner's hand I always offer them a few words of private congratulations while looking them in the eyes and shaking their hand. The process is very much like following the steps in a dance routine. Announce, shake their hand, look them in the eyes, congratulate them, step back, lead congratulations applause and lead the applause as they return to their seat. Repeat for the next winner.

Bridging between awards and recipients is essential to your performance. Remember... *it's not about you.*

You could give a brief personal example of how you have seen that the recipient has earned the award assuming you know them. Or you could give a brief overview of why you believe the award is important as you set up the next award to be delivered. The key word is *"brief."* Repeat the process.

Pitfalls to Avoid:

1. What happens if you announce the winner of an award and they are not present to accept it? One solution might be to ask the audience if there is anyone else from the individual's family or organization, if they are part of one, who would like to accept the award on their behalf. Perhaps if you are aware in advance of the reason, they are unable to attend an alternative action would be to call upon a leader in the hosting organization to accept the award in the absent winner's behalf.

2. If you are presenting awards of achievement and the recipient is not there to accept, do not give the award to someone with the directions of "Just give it to them next time that you see them." I have known of awards that have taken a year or more to get to their recipient. By the time that it did, the significance of the award had diminished.

3. You are presenting awards and notice the award you are giving isn't the one that is supposed to be next or there is a spelling mistake on the engraving. What do you do? I go with the principal of the "show must go on!" I would present the award and when the opportunity arises, I would mention to the recipient there was a slight problem but not to worry about it and we would solve it after the ceremony.

4. Photo ops can add a lively dimension to your ceremonies but what can you do when they take up too much time or are disruptive? As the Emcee, you are in charge of the proceedings. If you want to restrict the time allowed for each photo op, you can do so. There is nothing wrong with advising that the winner will be available for a photo opportunity upon conclusion of the formal ceremonies. You should offer your services for re-presenting the award at that time. Don't forget to smile!

5. What can be done about an award recipient whose acceptance speech never seems to end? If they are the one paying you, you might want to let them run on a little. If they aren't, and you are on a tight schedule, you may need to intervene. Often standing right beside the speaker can give them the hint that it is time to relinquish the spotlight. Sometimes it isn't. Sometimes you have to be forceful and interject with something along the lines of "in order to keep us on track to allow our other winners to speak, I'm going to have to cut you off"... I would then lead the applause and hopefully the speaker will get the hint.

12. WHAT SEATING ARRANGEMENT WORKS BEST FOR YOUR AUDIENCE?

As the Emcee, you may not have a lot of influence in how the meeting room or area will be set up. This will likely fall into the duties of the facility staff or perhaps the event organizer. The facility staff i.e. those that work in the venue will have experience with what works in their particular rooms. However, you as the Emcee have a vested interest in the success of the event and it would be prudent to take a close look at the room layout to identify any logistical challenges that the venue staff may not be aware of.

At a recent Toastmasters conference where I served as a Co-Chair, not the Emcee, my partner and I identified some problem areas with the room set-up the hotel usually used.

We had special needs of requiring the outer walls of the meeting room to be used for a head table, silent auction tables and a raised stage area for speech contests to be conducted. We also required all the tables to have a clear sight line of the head table on the right wall as well as the speaking stage on the back wall.

It was compounded by our requirement to have a clear path down the centre of the room to provide an unobstructed view of the stage so that a videographer could record the speaking contests.

This was a first for the hotel staff and they had to work with us to make this room configuration work for everyone. Not only did it have to ensure sight lines we had to consider the needs of those attendees who had self-identified as being hearing-impaired. We also had to consider traffic flow for both the conference attendees and the hotel's serving staff.

13. ADDITIONAL EMCEE DUTIES

I n this chapter we'll look at additional tasks or duties you may encounter in your role as an Emcee.

SPONSORS & PRESENTING DOOR PRIZES:

Announcing and plugging event sponsors throughout an event is standard fare as an Emcee. It can be challenging to fit the announcement into your agenda if it is tight. You need to be aware of unexpected opportunities that arise to fit an announcement in.

As the Emcee you may be required to present door prizes as part of the program. This activity works better if you have someone from the host organization to assist you. Better still, you announce it, and have the hosts handle the drawing for winners.

Announcing Procession to Buffet Lines:

Meals served in a buffet manner add an additional task to your Emcee roles. The challenge is to prevent a mass rush to the food tables, especially if your audience has worked up an appetite.

Usually in advance, the event organizers create a way of naming the tables that the guests are seated. You may find that the venue has set up a simple number system i.e. a number on a card set in a table standard. I have seen local geographical names used. Example: roads or mountains or even wineries or popular locally produced wines. Your task is to ensure that you have this info in advance of starting your other duties.

It can also be helpful to have someone from the catering staff signal you to indicate you can call up another table or two to the buffet line.

Depending on the nature of the event I have seen Emcees have contests to determine which table goes up next. There could be a task or a quick quiz that is offered and the winning table wins the prize of going up next.

Don't forget to arrange for someone to get a meal for you, otherwise you could go hungry!

Emergencies:

I previously described the Emcee role as being a facilitative one. There are times such as in an emergency, where your audience will look to you for leadership. As part of your pre-event preparation I would suggest you consult with the venue staff to find out where the fire escape routes are for your meeting room.

Most venues have an emergency plan in place and have set up designated staging areas i.e. places for people to gather away from the danger. Examples might be the South Parking Lot or perhaps the courtyard behind...

The venue may have different fire alarm rings for different codes. An intermittent ring or a chiming ring may mean a fire is present somewhere in the building however, you need to be aware of it but not necessarily have to evacuate at this time. A steady ring could mean that you are required to evacuate immediately.

Your role during times as this is to stay calm. You have the mic and therefore are in control. Audience members will look to you for direction or clarity. If it is necessary, provide directions telling them where the fire exits are and where they should exit to in an orderly fashion. It would seem obvious to say this but I will anyway… don't forget to look after your own personal safety. You are not the Captain of a ship and are not expected to be a hero.

Miscellaneous:

I am a firm believer in the Boy Scout motto of "Be Prepared!" I think being prepared for potential problems can go a long way in establishing your credibility of being a *master* of ceremonies.

For example, if you routinely bring a briefcase with you, it can be helpful to include an emergency kit of items that might be needed for managing from the stage. It could be extra batteries for handheld wireless mics. Duct tape for securing cables/power cords to the floor to prevent tripping. Scotch tape if paper needs to be repaired or something needs to be attached to a wall. Be careful with the tape though as many venues prohibit you using it on their walls.

Data Projectors & Powerpoint Presentation:

As the Emcee you may be responsible for the control and custody of a data projector, projecting various items such as the event's agenda.

While Powerpoint presentations and data projectors can be great to work with, they can also be troublesome.

I would suggest you test them out shortly before you go live to ensure they work. Then put them into a sleep mode, turning them back on again just before you go live.

14. BACK-UP PLANS

We mentioned back-up plans earlier in this book. A back-up plan comes in handy if an element of your plan/timeline fails. An example might be a scheduled speaker failing to show. Your task as the Emcee is to fill the gap or perhaps stall until someone else solves the problem.

Short unexpected gaps or delays in the timeline can be filled with promos for the event's sponsors or announcements the event organizers need to make. It would be prudent to have short stories or anecdotes you can deliver at these times. Your stories should be relevant to the theme of the meeting though. Many professional Emcees collect and develop small and large group activities that can help energize the group.

Here is an example of a large group activity that I have used occasionally, right after the meal was served and the award ceremony started.

"Wasn't that a great meal? Let's show our appreciation to our Catering staff!"

"We have been sitting for quite a while and we are going to be sitting for a while longer so now it is time for the aerobic exercise portion of our event. Did they forget to tell you about that when you registered?"

"I would like everyone to stand as you are able and give yourself a bit of room to move a bit."

"Move your arms around a few times to loosen up."

"Okay, now raise your arms up to shoulder height and together on the count of three I would like everyone to do one deep finger bend."

"One... two... three... bend!"

"Let's hear an applause!"

Upon completion of the exercise:

"Okay, is anybody winded from the exercise? Do we need to call an ambulance for anyone? I am a Registered Nurse trained in CPR so I can likely hold you over until the ambulance arrives. Everybody is good?

"And... I would like to thank you for that standing ovation! I really appreciate it!"

THIS LITTLE EXERCISE HAS ALWAYS BEEN WELL RECEIVED. I THINK ITS success lays in the fact the audience realizes they have been set up.

PART II

THE BUSINESS OF EMCEEING

15. OVERVIEW

I f you are reading this book because you have an event rapidly approaching and it is your task to emcee, the following section may not interest you.

At least not at this point in time. Once you have completed your emceeing assignment, you might very well say to yourself "Well, that wasn't so bad. I wonder if I can make some money at it?"

This section will be of interest to those who have been earning income as an emcee and would like to turn it into a business.

I take a different approach to developing a business than what others might. I'm going to be drawing from content from some of my other books to make my points.

One of the not so secret secrets I have learned about being successful in business is you can't work in a vacuum.

At one time it may have been a matter of "it's not who you know... it's who knows you."

Nowadays, it is a matter of "it's not who you know... it's who knows you know!"

You may be an excellent emcee, however if nobody knows it, you won't likely find a lot of engagements.

To be successful in business, you need to market and promote yourself. You need to advertise your service. You need to get out there and network with business professionals who may be in the position to engage your services.

Over the next few chapters we will look at self-promotion, marketing and networking. These can be described as soft skills that can either make or break your business venture.

Then after that we will look at the logistics of setting up your emceeing business.

16. INTRODUCTION TO NETWORKING

Networking to build your connections is an essential element in the development of your emcee business, or for that matter... any business.

While advertising your business is important in getting the word out to the world, many people prefer to do business with those they know, like and trust.

Some would call this doing business 'belly to belly.'

This is where networking comes in. I'm fond of a quote by John Jantsch, from Duct Tape Marketing... "Networking isn't something you do before work, or after work... it is work."

Another quote... I'm not sure from who goes "if you're not networking... you're not working."

Over the next few chapters we will explore some of the elements involved in successfully networking.

If you are interested in going into greater detail about networking I will recommend my book **Power Networking for Shy People: How to Network Like a Pro.** http://powernetworkingforshypeople.com

17. PERSONAL BRANDING

A few years ago I read a book by William Bridges... <u>**Creating You & Company: Learn to think like the CEO of your own company**</u>. He encourages you to market yourself as if <u>you</u> are the company. Blow your own horn! If you don't, who will?

This chapter's content is excerpted from another book I have under development entitled **Blow Your Own Horn: Marketing & Promotional Strategies for Business Professionals.**

BRANDING

Let's start off by determining what a brand is.

From Wikipedia...

A brand is a name, term, design, symbol, or other feature that distinguishes one seller's product from those of others.

Brands are used in business, marketing and advertising.

A brand is any name, design, style, words or symbols used singularly or in combination that distinguish one product from another in the eyes of the customer.

Branding is a set of marketing and communication methods that help to distinguish a company from competitors and create a lasting impression in the minds of customers.

The key components that form a brand's toolbox include a brand's identity, brand communication (such as logos and trademarks), brand awareness, brand loyalty and various brand management strategies.

We are all familiar with commercial branding and are likely bombarded with it every day. Coca Cola, Pepsi Cola and Nike readily come to mind.

These are well-established brands.

Personal Branding Defined

Again, according to Wikipedia, personal branding is the practice of people marketing themselves and their careers as brands.

Let's expand upon the concept of Personal Branding.

While previous self-help management techniques were about self-improvement, the personal-branding concept suggests instead that success comes from self-packaging.

The term is thought to have been first used and discussed in a 1997 article by Tom Peters.

Personal branding is essentially the ongoing process of establishing a prescribed image or impression in the mind of others about an individual, group, or organization.

Personal branding often involves the application of one's name to various products.

Athletes and celebrities come to mind.

If that is your situation, well good for you!

I would expect you have staff to look after you.

For the rest of us mere mortals, let's drill down a little.

So why don't we self-promote?

There are likely numerous reasons many of us don't like to talk about ourselves to others.

Many of us have likely been taught at a young age from our mothers that it is wrong to promote yourself.

"It is bragging and nobody likes braggarts!"

That may be a generalization and it really isn't fair to pick on mothers, considering all the good they do for us.

However, while many people likely don't like braggarts, it doesn't necessarily follow that talking about yourself in a favourable light... is bragging.

Walt Whitman was an American Cowboy poet, essayist and journalist, way back in the mid to late 1800s.

I'm fond of his quote about personal branding.

He probably didn't relate it any way to personal branding but here goes...

"If you done it... it ain't bragging!"

I think Walt hit the proverbial nail on the head. If you have done something and you talk about it, then it isn't bragging.

That sounds like self-promotion to me.

Can you think of any other reasons that we don't self-promote?

It could be a simple matter of we really don't know <u>how to</u> promote ourselves.

Through this chapter and upcoming chapters I'm hoping the strategies I provide will help resolve the problem if you identify with not knowing how to promote yourself.

As your skill in self-promotion increases and your self-confidence as well, you should find it easier to self-promote.

Another simple reason may be we don't have <u>time</u> to self-promote.

Then there is a simple reason that most of us have likely experienced at one time or another. It can be embarrassing at first when you create promotional copy, featuring yourself in a good light.

If you've written a resume lately, that's exactly what you had to do.

One of the features of social media platforms is they often require you to create a Bio or a Profile as a term of your membership.

While these can be a great opportunity for self-promotion, the first few times can be challenging.

Do you write your promotional copy in the first person as "I did this, this and this"?

Or do you write it in the 3rd person, "Rae Stonehouse, renowned best-selling author is known for..."?

Okay, so I'm not a best selling author yet, but I have a head-start on promoting it.

Before we move on to the next chapter, if you haven't done it recently, Google your name and see what comes up.

It is always a good idea to research yourself, just in case you have to do some damage control.

So... how do we self-promote?

18. WHAT DO YOU STAND FOR?

If you were asked to describe yourself in one word or perhaps a few, what would they be? If I were to ask a colleague or friend of yours the same question, would they offer the same words as yours?

If I were asked that question 10 to 15 years back I would say I was a catalyst. As a nurse therapist I helped my patients and fellow staff to move forward with problems in their lives that were holding them back.

I no longer serve in that manner in my job so I don't believe the word catalyst fits me anymore. Now the words creative, systematic, organized, loyal and persistent come to mind.

What word would you use to describe yourself?

Recently, I learned of an acronym that resonates with me. **H.O.P.E.**

Helping Other People Evolve. I may not be doing so in my nursing job right now but I certainly am a catalyst in the self-help books I write and publish and the systems and strategies I create. The words I used to describe myself ring true and serve me in helping others evolve.

So what words would you use to describe yourself? Do you <u>walk</u> your <u>talk</u>? Do others know what you stand for? Have you told them?

Maybe you should. That's all part of the blowing your own horn concept. People aren't mind readers. Sometimes you have to tell them what they *should* be thinking. That's called <u>marketing</u>.

It would also likely be a good idea to ask the people in your life what they believe you stand for. That's called <u>research</u>. Their answer may surprise you.

I will probably remember for the rest of my days, one example of a person who did not <u>walk</u> their talk. He was the keynote motivational speaker at a conference I attended and was promoting healthy living, being everything that you could be and leading by example. I observed him later that evening in the hotel's bar, pounding back the liquor and smoking like a chimney.

I think the message here is when you are developing your professional image you need to have it turned on at all times. In small communities, people you network with in business situations will likely encounter you at social get-togethers or at the grocery store.

19. DEVELOPING YOUR USP

Your **unique selling proposition** (a.k.a. **unique selling point,** universal selling point or **USP**) is a marketing concept used to differentiate yourself from your competitors or others in the marketplace.

Some good recent examples of products with a clear USP are:

- Head & Shoulders "You get rid of dandruff"

SOME UNIQUE PROPOSITIONS THAT WERE PIONEERS WHEN THEY WERE introduced:

- Dominoes Pizza: "You get fresh, hot pizza delivered to your door in 30 minutes or less--or it's free."
- Fed Ex: "When your package absolutely, positively has to get there overnight"
- M&Ms: "Melts in your mouth, not in your hand"
- Metropolitan Life: "Get Met, It Pays"

The term USP has been largely replaced by the concept of a **Positioning Statement**.

Positioning is determining what place a brand (tangible good or service) should occupy in the consumer's mind in comparison to its competition. A position is often described as the meaningful difference between the brand and its competitors. **Source:** Wikipedia

I recently was blindsided at a Chamber of Commerce function in my city when we were standing in circle participating in what they call a power networking session. We were asked what makes us or our business unique. I didn't recognize it as a USP question and provided an ineffective response. If I had recognized it for what it was i.e. a USP question, I would have responded with "Mr. Emcee is a full service event organizer. From start to finish... we do it all!"

Your challenge is to develop a USP that on one hand is short and to the point, yet is clear enough that it captures the essence of your business and will stick in the mind of whoever you are sharing it with. Having it prepared in advance, believing in it and being able to recite it with a moment's notice will go a long way in reducing your anxiety and fear which are all part of shyness.

I would also suggest researching your competitors or others in a similar business that are not necessarily your competitors to see if they have chosen a similar USP as you have. I am aware of two business coaches who chose a USP that had only one word that was different.

That one word totally changed the context of the USP but it really upset one of the coaches accusing the other of stealing her idea, even though they had been developed independent of each other.

20. HOW HIGH DOES YOUR ELEVATOR GO?

The buzzword for conducting business effectively in the new millennium may very well prove to be 'networking.' In turn, the key element of a networking interaction is the elevator pitch or elevator speech as some would call it. We used them as children... "you show me yours and I'll show you mine!"

Well, perhaps not quite the same but at its essence it's an opportunity to show your stuff and to learn about the other person. Assuming they follow the rules of course.

The basic premise is to imagine you are sharing an elevator ride with a person who could be influential in advancing your business or career. You have the duration of the elevator ride to impress upon this individual why they should buy into your cause or at least agree to talk to you some more about it.

How long should my elevator pitch be? Good question! Answer... It depends. Not much of an answer at first glance, but it really depends on the norms or the culture for location or venue of the networking session.

Presenting your 30-minute curriculum vitae wouldn't likely go over very well in a round-robin style of group introduction where the expectation is 30 seconds, not 30 minutes.

Many referral networking breakfast/luncheon groups based on the BNI (Business Networking International) model, limit their members to 30 second elevator pitches. The more members, the longer the activity takes, but at least it gives everyone an opportunity to speak.

A few years back I organized a series of Power Networking Breakfasts. It was speed networking at its best, very much like a speed dating concept. Participants were allowed two minutes and thirty seconds to deliver their pitch. Time limits were rigidly followed with Toastmasters style speech timing lights, green, amber and red and a bell to signal the speaker to stop their pitch, then on to the next pitcher. The pre-event promotional material advised the participant to come prepared with a two minute elevator pitch and to be prepared to answer a question or two about their pitch.

It was amazing to find that many of the participants faced challenges in trying to fill their two minutes. They had been programmed to stand up and speak and sit down within the restriction of 30 seconds.

I believe one of the challenges many of us face is we have been taught from an early age not to brag about ourselves. When it comes to business, if we don't promote ourselves or our business i.e. blow our own horn, then who will?

We should be passionate about our businesses and be able to talk at length about what we do, why we do it and why you should do business with us. In fact, I would challenge you to be prepared to deliver a 30-minute presentation about yourself and/or your business. Arguably that would likely be one of the slowest elevator rides ever, but if you have ever found yourself stuck in one for an extended period, you will know it could very well happen.

A challenge I have faced is with having multiple business ventures, volunteer roles, my professional career & pursuits, I could easily take the full thirty minutes for my 30-second pitch allotment. That doesn't leave any room for the others. If you find yourself in a similar situation, I think that the answer lays in referring back to our analogy of the elevator ride.

Many larger highrises have more than one elevator. I would challenge you to create multiple elevator pitches you can use to match with the appropriate venue and situation. A social setting may be a good place to talk about some activities you are involved with and touching upon, but not going heavily into what you do for a living.

At a Toastmasters conference I would likely introduce myself as...

"Good morning everyone, I'm Rae Stonehouse. I'm a Distinguished Toastmaster and have been a member for over twenty-five years. So far! I've served as our District 21 Governor a few years back and continue to serve our leaders in multiple roles. My passion is organizing and creating something from nothing. I'd love to hear how your Toastmasters experience has been. Rae Stonehouse."

I've kept it short and sweet and hopefully have piqued someone's interest that they would want to talk to me some more. I haven't mentioned my profession or my business ventures at all. I will likely fit that into the follow-up conversation as the opportunity arises.

Here's an example of an elevator pitch that wouldn't be such a good idea. Let's say I was in a meeting of the senior managers in my organization. It would probably not be well received if I were to give an introductory pitch highlighting my experience as a union activist. It would be much better to identify my name, my professional designation, where I work, how long and what I bring to the table.

I'm a firm believer in the adage "If the only tool you have in your toolbox is a hammer, then every problem will be a nail." I believe that to be an effective networker you need to have a selection of tools in your metaphorical toolbox. Having a selection of elevator pitches to be able to rely on for any situation is one such tool. Don't throw away that hammer though. Sometimes a hammer is exactly what is needed!

21. DEVELOPING YOUR ELEVATOR PITCH

You need to develop your elevator pitch like you would a formal presentation. Just because you are introducing yourself conversationally in a 1 to 1 or a small group doesn't mean you should wing it.

Preparation is the key to your success. Remember, you should be prepared for different lengths of elevator rides and different situations.

Follow these steps to develop your unique pitch.

DESCRIBE YOURSELF AS A SOLUTION TO A PROBLEM:

The most important part of your elevator pitch is your opening sentence. You need to grab your audience's attention by telling what is unique about what you do.

In your very first sentence you need to say your name, your business' name and describe yourself as a solution to the problems your clients, customers or business associates face. Listeners don't usually care about your job title as much as what you can do for them.

When creating the first line of your elevator pitch, put yourself in the audience's shoes and answer the age old question "What's in it for me?"

A superior elevator pitch increases your heart rate. It speaks to who you really are and what excites you about your business. If you don't get excited about it, who will?

YOUR PITCH NEEDS TO ADDRESS THE FIVE Ws:

The first step is to develop answers to the following questions:

1. What does your business do? (For example, begin your answer with "We provide...")
2. Whom does your business do it for? (For example, begin your answer with "For small and mid-sized healthcare providers.")
3. Why do they care? Or, What's in it for them? (For example, include in your answer "so that they can...," "who can no longer afford...," or "who are tired of...")
4. Why is your business different? (For example, begin your answer with "As opposed to..." or "Unlike...")
5. What is your business? (For example, begin your answer with "My business is an insurance against...")

Don't forget to include your **USP**, your hook. It is a good way to close off your elevator pitch. For example, using my business... "Mr. Emcee Your Okanagan Event Planner of Choice. From start to finish... we do it all!"

TELL AN ANECDOTE: (FOR LONGER PITCHES):

After you describe the problems you solve, tell a short story to explain your motivation for doing what you do. This story should be something exciting... the aha! moment where you realized that you had to do what you do. Or you could tell a story that illustrates how exceptionally good you are at your craft.

Start a dialogue:

Conclude your pitch with an open-ended question... one that can't be answered with a simple "yes" or "no" answer. Closing with a question can draw the listener in, serving as a foundation for a deeper conversation and collaboration, and eventually, a relationship.

Make sure you prepare, rehearse and regularly revise your elevator pitch to effectively market yourself and capitalize on opportunities that come your way --- whether you are in an elevator or not!

Here are some important considerations to keep in mind.

- Don't confuse people with your pitch. No one needs to hear your entire work history on first meeting you.
- No matter how tough it's been you don't need to tell a sob story, paint a positive picture. You need to be congruent with your professional image. As they say you need to **walk your talk**. If you are marketing yourself as a wellness coach it would not work for you if you were sick quite often or were carrying 20 to 30 extra pounds.

22. ELEVATOR PITCH TEMPLATE

Here is an easy-to-use elevator pitch template you can use to develop you own.

OPENING SALUTATION: (GOOD MORNING, GOOD AFTERNOON, GOOD evening)

Your Name:

Your Business Name:

USP: (what is unique about what you do?)

(How are you a solution to the problem?

Closing Comments: (Repeat your name & business name and add a hook)

** For longer time allowances factor in an anecdote and/or close by starting a dialogue.

An example of a short elevator pitch I have used is as follows:

"Hello everyone. I am Rae Stonehouse aka Mr. Emcee and I am a cat juggler! Metaphorically of course! As an event organizer and promoter I have multiple cats in the air at the same time. Sometimes they go the way they are supposed to, most of the time they don't. My job is to make those cats fly in formation. I provide organization for the many details that accompany an event and provide my clients peace of mind. Unless they have an allergy to cats of course. Rae Stonehouse... Mr. Emcee... your Okanagan Valley event organizer & promoter of choice. From start to finish... we do it all!"

23. USING TECHNOLOGY TO YOUR ADVANTAGE

YOUR E-MAIL SIGNATURE
A relatively easy way of promoting yourself is to develop an e-mail signature file that not only provides your contact information, it also allows you to promote yourself. E-mail signatures can easily be set up using Outlook, assuming you are using Outlook and a word processing program.

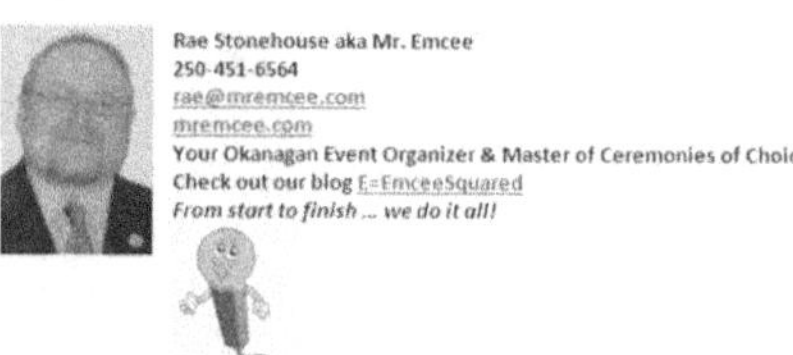

YOUR SIGNATURE FILE IS LIKE A SMALL BILLBOARD THAT PROMOTES YOU. You should make it as easy as possible for people to contact you. If you have a website, provide the url so the reader of your e-mail can easily navigate to it. Make sure it has been hyperlinked i.e. when they click on the link it will take them to the website.

I am not currently using it on any of my signature files but many people insert a link to their Linkedin profile if they feel that there is value in doing so.

Don't forget to add a head-shot photo of yourself. I expand on the subject elsewhere in this book. I often get the comment "Oh, I recognize you from your e-mail." For a shy networker this can be quite helpful. In theory, people will walk up to you and say "I know you!"

24. BUSINESS CARD PRESENTATION & ETIQUETTE

I f you are planning on some serious networking, you should have business cards available to present. Not having a card may be a missed opportunity for you. Besides serving as an introduction for you and your business they will serve as a visual prompt to remind the other person they met and spoke to you.

Business cards are quite inexpensive to print nowadays, so cost shouldn't be a deterrent to having some printed. If you are in transition and expect your info to change soon, your printer will likely accommodate small batch runs.

Even if you are technically not in business, perhaps in transition and looking for employment, you should still have a card that outlines who you are and what you do or the kind of work that you are looking for and how someone can get in contact with you.

Some business people believe in having their photo as part of the card. Supposedly, I'm guessing here, so you remember them better. It can be problematic if they have used a more youthful picture from yesteryear. We joke about some realtor's (real estate agents) business cards and newspaper advertisements we see locally. Their public marketing image is a young youthful person and when you meet them they are somewhat prune looking i.e. dried up and aged! I feel I have been tricked. Vanity can affect people in different ways I suppose.

The Japanese take business card presentation in a one-to-one networking situation far more serious than we do. To them, ritual is involved. When presented with a business card you are expected to accept it with both hands, hold it in front of you and read the content of the card, both sides. You would then hold it with respect as the other person shares their elevator pitch. You would only place it in your pocket after you had left the person and you would never deface the card by writing on it.

In North America we are a little less respectful. Sometimes, quite a bit! I have met a fellow who within the first seconds of meeting him he announces "Well let's get this out of the way" and hands me his card. I expect that he wasn't as comfortable or skilled at networking as he thought he was.

I have also seen an influential woman walk up to a group of people and start passing out her business cards. "Here you go, one for you and one for you!" She then left the group and went over to another and repeated the process. It was like she was feeding chickens or passing out candy to children who were trick or treating at her door. The purpose of passing out her business card seemed to be missed. I wonder if she was actually shy and was covering up her uncomfortableness?

So what is the correct way to present your card to another? How and when?

I'm sure everybody has their own view on the matter.

When I have been offered another's business card as part of an introduction that is under way, I will adopt what I described earlier as the Japanese method. I will accept it, quickly read the details and I will keep it in my hand in full view. I see the offering of a business card from another as the cue to offer mine in return. I often make a comment about a detail or an aspect of their business card to rein-force that I have taken a serious look at it.

If I don't see any action from my partner towards offering their busi-ness card, I will initiate it myself. Asking, "Do you have a business card?" can be easier than saying "Here is my business card." Of course, their providing a card opens it up for me to provide mine.

I will also listen for a verbal cue of "I should get in contact with you", "I will keep in touch" or anything close to that as a signal for me to offer my card.

In an earlier chapter I mentioned the value of having different elevator pitches available for a given situation. At a business networking event I am prepared to give business cards as the discus-sion develops. After getting my own cards mixed up far too many times with the cards that I have received I have developed my own system of organization.

I usually wear a blazer with hip pockets. In my left pocket I would have a supply of my business cards. In my right pocket I have, a card representing my role as the Chairman of the Board of our local entre-preneurs society. In my wallet, I will carry some cards that I can pass out related to Toastmasters.

When I receive a <u>new</u> business card, after reading it I will insert it into my shirt pocket. As I have several blazers or suit coats I organize them all the same way. We will talk about name badges elsewhere, but I carry one in each blazer so that it will be there when I need it.

If I am expecting to pass out more than the average amount of busi-ness cards at an event, I will have an extra supply in my briefcase or my vehicle should I require them.

A female reader of the last paragraph pointed out to me "What if you are wearing a little black dress and carrying a clutch purse where do you put the cards that you have collected?" Having never worn a "little black dress" I can only assume they don't include deep pockets.

Perhaps wearing the dress in the first place to a business networking event might be the point to focus on. I make no proclamation of being an expert on women's fashion!

I will even muddy the water a little and ask "Should you give your business card in all situations?"

I've been in interactions where the other individual doesn't seem overly interested in me, or are overly interested in themselves. I may make a judgement call on the spot and choose not to share my business card.

Then there are those who choose <u>not</u> to share business cards. This could be a simple matter of not having their cards printed yet or having problems deciding what to put on the card. Not everybody is creative.

I've heard of one woman who when asked for her business card replies "Oh, I don't do business cards. I prefer to write down the person's name and contact information on my little pad. It's much more personal."

It may be more personal to her, but in today's fast-paced world, this could be an irritant or an imposition to some networkers.

I'm reminded of a young fellow who attended one of my speed networking events I mentioned earlier. He was a salesman for a high-end office furniture business. When I asked him why he didn't have any business cards he replied "How could anybody forget this smiling face?"

Well, apparently they did. The next time I saw him he was behind the counter of our local Dairy Queen filling ice cream cones.

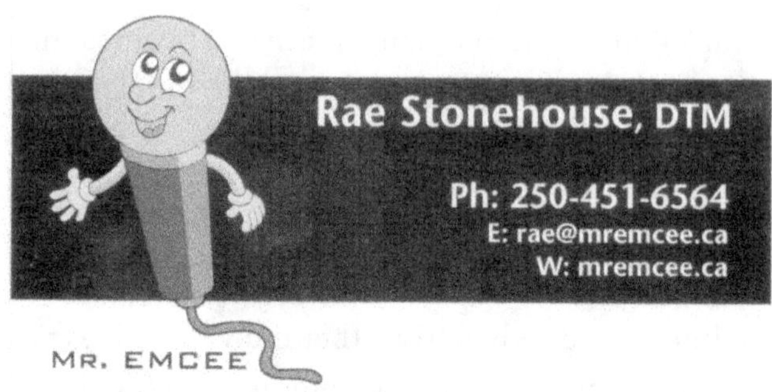

Need a Master of Ceremonies for your event?

From start to finish
we do it all!

ASK Us

25. WEAR A NAME TAG

Many networking events you attend will provide a sticky-backed name tag with something like "Hello, my name is..." If the organizers are insistent that you wear it, I would suggest you write your name as interestingly as you can, something that will attract another to focus on it.

My preference would be to wear a name badge that professionally displays my name and my business/organization. I believe people tend to scan your name badge when they are first approaching you to see if there is an immediate connection between you and them.

They can also look at it while they are speaking to you to keep your name in their mind. It can also help as a reminder to yourself if you get to the point where you are so overwhelmed with other's names and the networking process that you can look down and remind yourself what yours is.

Here are a couple badges I had made for my wife and me for my business. I purchased two for myself so I could keep one in each of my sports jacket. I was surprised at how inexpensive they were to purchase i.e. $45.00 for three badges.

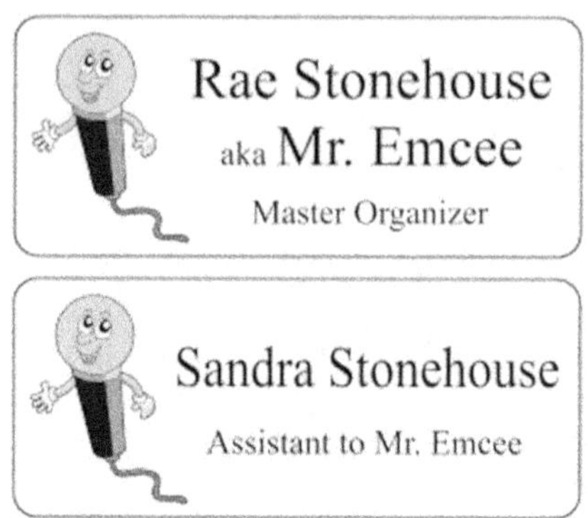

IN THIS CASE, THE TERM MASTER ORGANIZER, SETS SOMEBODY UP FOR the inevitable question of "So what do you organize?"

26. WHOLE LOTTA SHAKIN GOIN ON

A handshake is more than just a greeting. It is also a message about your personality and confidence level. In business, a handshake is an important tool in making the right first impression.

Before extending your hand, introduce yourself. Extending your hand should be part of an introduction, not a replacement for using your voice. This isn't the cue to start reciting your elevator pitch though. Extending your hand without saying anything may make you appear nervous or overly aggressive.

On one hand (pun intended!) it would seem that shaking someone's hand should be an easy process. We have likely been doing it most of our adult life. On the other hand, some people seem to have problems with it.

I believe part of the problem that creates anxiety is we over think things sometimes. We are anxious because we give more importance to the activity than it really deserves, and it takes on a life of its own... creating anxiety. A self-fulfilling prophesy if there ever was one.

Another part that likely creates anxiety is we can only control our portion of the interaction. If our partner is an experienced hand-shaker, then all should go smoothly but many aren't.

There are a few different hand-shaking styles that come up in the literature and I am sure you have likely experienced them yourselves.

I personally don't like grasping someone's hand who has the so-called '**wet fish**' handshake. It can leave you with an obsessive urge to wipe your hand as soon as you can, but fight the urge.

Even worse, there are times my hand is sweating and I don't want the label. I have developed the habit of giving my hand a quick, unobtrusive wipe on my pant leg before offering my hand.

Then there is '**bone-crusher Bill.**' The offered hand often comes in as a curve from the hip of Bill with the express purpose of crushing walnuts. Or so it would seem. Bill never realizes the pain he causes in others or the fact people start to avoid him. Word can get around!

Another ineffective handshake I call the '**royal**' handshake. Someone only offers you the tips of their fingers and no matter how hard you try you can't seem to grasp more than a few fingers. You are left feeling that you were robbed.

The bottom line is to avoid being any of these profiles. If you need to practice at home before going to a networking session, do so.

It seems to becoming more common that friends are hugging when meeting in a social setting. There are many people I call "huggy" people. I would suggest waiting to see if you are offered one rather than expecting one. It could make for an awkward situation if you were to offer a hug on a first contact and have it rejected.

27. FOLLOW-UP IS EVERYTHING

It can be a great feeling when coming home from a networking event and looking at the stack of business cards you have collected. You even spoke at length to many of the card-donators. Some, it can be a little difficult to recall who they actually were.

"Now was he the tall fellow with the bad hair piece... or was he...?" You've probably experienced that scenario more than once. And you know what... perhaps some of the business people you gave your precious business card to are thinking something similar. Hopefully not about your bad hair though.

For effective business networking I recommend the quality over quantity method. Some would say that networking is a numbers game, the more you meet the higher the chances of your meeting someone who can benefit you. Take, for example, you are meeting someone for the first time and if the setting and conditions permit, they deliver their elevator pitch and you return with yours. Then comes the awkward moment, what to say next. You can either carry on conversing about something of no consequence "Nice day, eh?" until one of you tires or you can explore common interests.

Assuming you have a common interest I would suggest you take the lead in the conversation in getting the other to expand upon the commonality or something they had previously said.

Many networkers make the mistake of trying to sell their product or themselves at the initial meeting. Your goal at that juncture should be to arrange to meet them at another time, perhaps for coffee, to discuss those common areas further.

Even though many of us are electronically connected to our offices with our smart phones and can likely check to see if we are available at a certain date and time to make a coffee date, we probably won't. When you suggest meeting for coffee, later, if the person is willing to set up a date and time, on the spot, I would go with it. Location can always be determined later by e-mail.

If they aren't willing to set a time and date, I would refer to their business card and say something to the effect of "Can I reach you at this e-mail? I'll contact you next week and see if we can set up a time to get together for a quick coffee."

Unfortunately, for many networkers, this is as far as they go. They don't do the follow-up. Life gets busy, there is always one more thing to do with your business and before you know it you have lost the window of opportunity. There is a strong possibility the individual you were networking with also has a list of people they are following up with and other commitments. It is far too easy to get left by the wayside if you don't take action to stand out from the others.

At a morning meeting of a breakfast networking group I belonged to we discussed the issue of follow up. A member related that in his experience, if you actually follow-up with a lead, it puts you way ahead of those that don't. He makes a practice of following up with a networking connection within three days of the original meeting and says it is amazing how many people have said "You know, you are one of the few that actually follows up." Yes, following up can help you stand out from the competition.

The coffee get together is the opportunity for each of you to share your business details and determine if there is enough reason to continue at another time to develop your relationship further and ideally to do business together.

You might ask "I've contacted them three times by e-mail and even left a couple voice mails but they haven't gotten back to me. What do I do next?"

There could be a legitimate reason for them not getting back to you. Life happens! But they could be acting non-assertively and are actively avoiding you. I would have to respond with "If that was true, is that someone you really want to network with or to do business with?"

If you are to continue, it could easily label you as a stalker.

One suggestion may be to add them to your tickler file. A couple weeks down the road, ignoring the fact they haven't acknowledged you yet, you would be justified in sending them a message something like "I just noticed we didn't get together a few weeks ago like we said we would. Where did the time go? It seems to be picking up speed. Last time we met we were discussing our common interests of... Are you still interested in getting together?" If you still don't receive a response, I would put them in the "inactive" file.

When it comes to networking, to stand out from your competition, remember to follow-up.

28. SOCIAL MEDIA IS HERE TO STAY

Social media is here to stay. At least until the next latest and greatest bright shiny object comes along.

Developing an on-line presence and leveraging social media can be a great strategy in in expanding your on-line reach.

A quick on-line search to answer the question "what social media is good for networking?" revealed: Linkedin, Twitter and Instagram as being extraordinary tools for expanding and deepening your connections with business contacts, clients and potential partners.

FIVE TIPS TO NETWORKING THROUGH SOCIAL MEDIA ARE COMMONLY identified:

- Build a social presence
- Post engaging content
- Avoid the hard sell
- Focus on quality over quantity
- Practice good etiquette.

Having been on social media for a while now I agree with the five points. In fact, they seem to be rather self-evident to me.

While I whole-heartedly agree with Linkedin being recognized as a good on-line networking platform, maybe even the best, I don't agree with the suggestion of Twitter and Instagram being used for networking.

The development of different social media platforms and the ability to use them to market products or services has totally changed the face of marketing.

Traditional marketing has had to absorb the new concept of on-line marketing. Many traditional marketers have had to incorporate on-line marketing strategies to stay in business. A plethora of self-proclaimed marketing experts has been the result. Many of them will tell you that you absolutely need to be on social media and they have the skills and time to do it for you. For a fee of course!

Leveraging social media is now within the reach of mere mortals. While I agree that Twitter, Instagram and Facebook for that matter, provide value in promoting yourself, your products and your service, I don't agree with their value in networking.

Sure, you can connect with a lot of people and it looks impressive that you have a massive number of connections but I ask 'are you really networking?'

I question the value of these connections. Twitter has evolved into a one-way data dump where everybody is pushing their content. As for meaningful conversations on Twitter, as far as I'm concerned... it's a joke.

I think Facebook is a great place to promote yourself however, I have many 'best friends' I have never met and am not likely to.

I'm sure there are a lot of social media enthusiasts who will disagree with me. If you disagree with me, try asking some of your on line friends for a loan and see what happens.

. . .

IN THE NEXT CHAPTER WE DIG INTO USING LINKEDIN TO DEVELOP YOUR network.

29. ARE YOU LINKEDIN?

Are you Linkedin? Well, you should be!

[This chapter is excerpted from my **Power Networking for Shy People: How to Network Like a Pro** book, if you are wondering about the shyness references. The content easily applies to those who aren't shy.]

Linkedin and the internet in general are a boon to shy networkers. The on-line world is a great leveller when it comes to the shy and introverted vs. the extroverted. When you are reading text on a website or elsewhere, the personality of the author doesn't usually show. I believe many introverts have better computer and technological skills than our extroverted colleagues. I believe our ability to focus on matters and our preference to work alone works in our favour.

You can research a person you want to connect to without ever having to leave the comfort of your home. Mobile apps on your smart phone also mean you can research somebody when you are out and about. You don't have to wait until you are in front of your desktop computer of laptop for that matter.

I used to describe Linkedin as being like your resume on steroids.

The content I had uploaded to my profile was very much in the curriculum vitae style of a resume. It seemed to go on and on when you were reading it. I had added every notable achievement to my list of accomplishments. The fact I was involved with and had lots of experience from many organizations as well as my professional career as a Registered Nurse, made it confusing.

There are seven elements of Linkedin I want to focus on in this section that are helpful to anyone starting and growing a business.

YOUR PERSONAL MARKETING AGENCY:

One of the first steps to take after opening your Linkedin account is to start to develop your **Profile**. Your profile connects you with others in your Linkedin network. As a new connection is made, often the new contact will go to your profile to learn more about you. Even people you have known for years will check you out. Imagine the number one thought going through someone's mind as they read your profile is... "Is there an opportunity for me to do business with this person?"

PARTS OF THE PROFILE:

Your Name: You have the option of having your name displayed fully or with your first name and last initial. Example: Rae Stonehouse vs Rae S. If you are using Linkedin as a business growth strategy it is suggested you use your full name.

Headline: Provide a descriptive headline statement. It does not need to be your current job title, although many people use this field in that way. Something that gives a glimpse into your uniqueness or personality can help you stand out from your competitors.

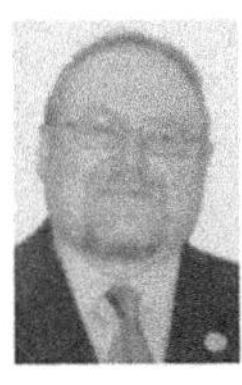

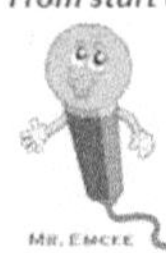

Rae Stonehouse aka Mr. Emcee
250-451-6564
rae@mremcee.com
mremcee.com
Your Okanagan Event Organizer & Master of Ceremonies of Choice
Check out our blog E=EmceeSquared
From start to finish ... we do it all!

In the **Background** heading you can add a **Summary** of your experience and what you currently have to offer. Under **Experience** you can add any experience you want highlighted. This is a good place to highlight your strengths and accomplishments. You can add bulleted points in this section, but it should not be all bullet points. Write your summary as if you are speaking conversationally to the person reading it.

It might be helpful to take a look at some other Linkedin user profiles to see how they have completed their profile. Every connection you gain won't necessarily be a business prospect for you. However, as you write your profile, you should do so with the intent a prospect will read it.

This is the place to blow your own horn! Make sure you highlight what you want the reader to see and to remember. Some people take a factual or chronological approach to creating their profile, others, more of a promotional or marketing one. My original profile included references to my nursing career and was designed for the possibility of using it for job search purposes. As I am approaching the end of my nursing career and moving into other ventures, I have removed references to my profession in favour of my entrepreneurial ventures and my volunteer life.

As an aside, the graphic illustrated above was an earlier version of what I had posted as my Linkedin profile.

I was at a meeting of my morning breakfast club where I was promoting my emcee business. A fellow member took me aside and advised me that he and a colleague had looked at my Linkedin profile and his colleague advised he wouldn't hire me based on my too casual photo.

While I see myself as being a casual person, I saw the value in updating my photo to a more professional one, which I did.

The irony was the fellow who brought this to my attention was dressed in flamboyant golf shorts and top... at a professional business meeting.

HERE ARE SOME GENERAL TIPS:

- Capitalize properly. "mary smith" is less professional than "Mary Smith."
- Proofread, proofread, proofread
- Avoid industry jargon as much as possible
- Avoid acronyms. If you must use them, explain the acronym in the first appearance of it in your profile. Example: ASAP (as soon as possible)
- Use a professional headshot photo of yourself for your profile. More about that later.

An earlier version of my Linkedin profile (see below) was written tongue-in-cheek. It had the following opening sentences:

<<How many people can honestly say that they spent part of their formative years in a maximum security hospital for the criminally insane?

Rae can! True, he was working as a staff in the Dietary Department and was able to go home every evening at the end of his shift but that experience has had a lasting effect on him.

Over the past 30+ years Rae has been working as a Registered Nurse, predominantly in the field of mental health/psychiatric nursing.>>

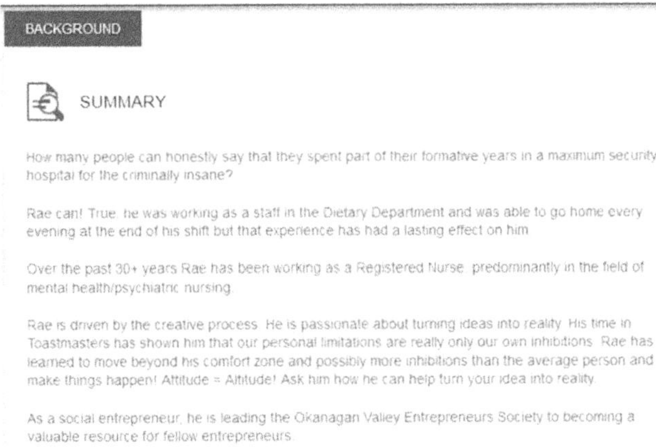

BACKGROUND

SUMMARY

How many people can honestly say that they spent part of their formative years in a maximum security hospital for the criminally insane?

Rae can! True, he was working as a staff in the Dietary Department and was able to go home every evening at the end of his shift but that experience has had a lasting effect on him.

Over the past 30+ years Rae has been working as a Registered Nurse, predominantly in the field of mental health/psychiatric nursing.

Rae is driven by the creative process. He is passionate about turning ideas into reality. His time in Toastmasters has shown him that our personal limitations are really only our own inhibitions. Rae has learned to move beyond his comfort zone and possibly more inhibitions than the average person and make things happen! Attitude = Altitude! Ask him how he can help turn your idea into reality.

As a social entrepreneur, he is leading the Okanagan Valley Entrepreneurs Society to becoming a valuable resource for fellow entrepreneurs.

In this version I had taken a promotional approach many would find uncomfortable in using. It didn't seem to have held me back any for those who have wanted to connect with me.

Currently I am using a more formalized profile overview, yet still promotional in nature.

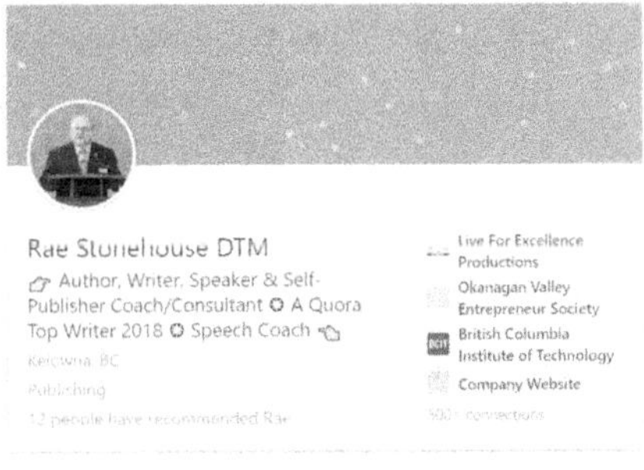

RAE A. STONEHOUSE IS A CANADIAN BORN AUTHOR & SPEAKER.

His professional career as a Registered Nurse working predominantly in psychiatry/mental health, has spanned four decades.

Rae has embraced the principal of CANI (Constant and Never-ending Improvement) as promoted by thought leaders such as Tony

Robbins and brings that philosophy to each of his publications and presentations.

Rae has dedicated the latter segment of his journey through life to overcoming his personal inhibitions. As a 25+ year member of Toastmasters International he has systematically built his self-confidence and communicating ability.

He is passionate about sharing his lessons with his readers and listeners. His publications thus far are of the self-help, self-improvement genre and systematically offer valuable sage advice on a specific topic.

His writing style can be described as being conversational. As an author Rae strives to have a one-to-one conversation with each of his readers, very much like having your own personal self-development coach.

Rae is known for having a wry sense of humour that features in his publications.

To learn more about Rae A. Stonehouse, visit the Wonderful World of Rae Stonehouse at http://raestonehouse.com or 250-451-6564

Specialties:

➤ Author of self-help books & on-line courses

➤ Speech presentation coaching & training

➤ Communicating & leadership skill development

➤ Keynote, workshop, seminar presenting & writing

➤ Facilitating/group moderating

➤ Website development & maintenance (Joomla & Wordpress)

➤ Recognized as a Top Writer 2018 at Quora for over 700 answers & 750,000 answer views

. . .

ANOTHER FEATURE TO ADD TO YOUR PROFILE IS **HONOURS & AWARDS**. If you have some and they are related to your profession or business venture, this is the place to promote them. I wouldn't recommend listing your first place bowling trophy unless you happen to be a professional bowler and you wanted people to be aware of the fact.

You can also promote **Publications** you have created and/or published as well as websites you have created or are associated with.

As you build your network, you can solicit **Recommendations** from people you have assisted in some capacity or conducted business with. These are testimonials that can prove to be quite powerful in helping someone who has come upon your name when they have been researching a specific search term in making a decision to contact you or not. You in turn, can provide recommendations for others you have worked with.

As you build your network it is worth your while to provide testimonials for other Linkedin members you have worked with, assuming you have something positive to say about them of course! The Law of Reciprocity often kicks in when you do so. When you submit a recommendation that has been unsolicited by another, they often feel obligated and create and submit a testimonial on your behalf in return.

Skills & Endorsements is a category Linkedin seems to believe has great value. I believe it would work against you if you didn't have anything in this area however, whether it benefits you in any way, I don't think so.

Whereas **Recommendations** requires some thought by the contributor, the **Skills & Endorsements** only require a click by the endorser. I've been highly recommended by connections I have never met and am unlikely to ever meet. Where is the value... or the credibility for that matter of these endorsements?

With a little work you can create a Linkedin profile that grabs the interest of the reader and has a higher chance of creating an opportunity. Something to remember is the search engines will not only index and post your Linkedin profile, but it will often link you with everyone you are linked to.

For example, if a person is searching for someone you are linked to and they have used their name as the search criteria, there is a high chance your name will appear in the search results for the other person. Your chances of being found in the search engines increase even more if you have chosen your keywords in your personal profile carefully.

So why bother doing this much work? A big part of networking is being visible. If people don't know you, they won't likely do business with you.

As an event planner working with small business owners and entrepreneurs I used the Linkedin Search feature quite frequently to target my search for whatever field or profession I was looking for.

When I am invited by somebody to connect with them in Linkedin, the first things I check out is their photo, their profile and the number of people they have connected to.

I tend to be suspicious when I see only a small amount of content posted under their Profile. Either they are just starting to create their profile, they are too lazy to upload the content, they really don't buy into the concept of sharing personal info on Linkedin or perhaps they are paranoid and don't want to share anything. Could be any of those reasons but I as the visitor to your site shouldn't have to jump to conclusions as to why they don't have much content posted.

Another area I find problematic is the photos people post of themselves. Your photo is an extension of your personal or business marketing plan. Save the cutesy photos of your dog or a close up of your eye or nose for Facebook. In fact posting a logo or a picture of your pet could get you kicked off Linkedin as it is against the rules and is listed in their terms of reference. I want to see what the person looks like if I am going to consider working with them.

As children, we were advised not to judge a book by its cover. Yet, we do it all the time. You only have about two to three seconds to make a good first impression with someone who checks out your profile with the possibility of doing business with you. Do you really want to waste that opportunity?

It can be your personal Research Department:

Once your profile is posted, you are able to start connecting with other members.

The Basic Linkedin package anyone can get for free includes a few features that can aid your research.

You can search for people, jobs, companies, by inserting text into the text box and clicking on the Add new search icon graphic.

Linkedin originally had a feature that allowed you to do an Advanced Search. With their moving to a revenue-raising model, sadly this is no longer available for free. You can still access it however, as the saying goes "it'll cost you!"

An additional search technique is to search for the individual through your favourite search engine. Linkedin and Facebook profiles seem to get indexed quite readily. With many people sharing the same name, ensure that you have the identified the correct person.

If you are taking your emcee business to the next level, there may be value in signing up for a Linkedin Company Page. Doing so allows you to expand upon your emcee business' branding, which may or may not be the same as your personal branding.

One challenge I have noted with building your contacts in this new format i.e. separate from your personal, is in name recognition.

While many people may recognize your personal name, they may not recognize your business name.

When you send out invitations to connect to people, you know or are currently connected to, you would be well-advised to add a personal note informing them about how you are connected and the fact you have a business that may be of value to them.

30. REACH OUT AND LINK SOMEBODY

A network is composed of more than one person. If you don't reach out and invite somebody to connect, or you don't receive any invitations to connect, then you don't really have a network.

Sending out an invitation to another Linkedin member can be a challenge for many shy people. We can tend to second guess ourselves... "Why would anyone want to connect with me?"

The Linkedin program will automatically send you notifications of people you might know and ask you whether you would like to connect with them. This can be a double-edged sword as the saying goes.

On one side, if you are connected with somebody, Linkedin will send you a list of names of people they are connected to and ask you if you would like to invite them to connect. If the names presented are people, you know already and they would know you, by all means send them an invitation to connect.

The other edge of the sword comes into play when you submit an invitation to somebody you know and they respond to the invitation with the answer they don't know you.

A few years back, while using the Linkedin app on my Iphone, I was sending out numerous invitations to connect with people who I thought would recognize my name only to find that Linkedin decided to punish me.

Apparently if too many people say they don't recognize you it triggers something in the system that takes away your privilege to send out an invitation to people you are connected with. At the time, while seemingly being punished for what Linkedin encouraged me to do, I had the extra step of having to add the individual's e-mail address as part of my invitation to connect.

Here is a list of tips to prevent restrictions from the Linkedin site:

- Invite only people you personally know.
- Invite only those you'd recommend to others.
- Personalize your invitation message. Explain how you know them or why you want to connect.
- Add a current head-shot photo to your profile so people recognize you.
- Use an InMail or Introduction if you don't know someone's email address. (these are currently paid features)
- Use the **Ignore** button for invitations from someone you know but choose not to connect with.
- Only use the 'I Don't Know' option when you truly don't know the member.

31. SEND MESSAGES OUT

Linkedin has added the sending e-mail out feature to several of their paid subscriptions.

However, there is limited ability in the free subscription to send out a message to members of groups you belong to.

You can send a message to a group member without being connected and adjust your **Member Message** settings from within the group.

To send a free message to a group member:

1. Click **Groups** at the top of your home page.
2. Click the group's name.
3. Click the **Members** tab
4. Move your cursor over the member's name and click the **Send message** link revealed on the right.
5. This link will appear if the member's settings allow them to be contacted by other group members.
6. Create your message and click **Send Message.**

Note: You can also click on a member's picture from the **Discussions** page and then click **Message.**

To view or adjust your **Member Messages** settings:

1. Click **Groups** at the top of your home page.
2. Click the group's name.
3. Click the group's **...** tab.
4. Click **Update Your Settings**.
5. Next to **Messaging**, check or uncheck the box next to choose whether group members in your extended network can message you.

Note: Contact information isn't shared when you use the **Send message** link though groups. Messages they send on your behalf only show the name on your account.

32. CREATE A DATABASE OF CONNECTIONS

I suggested in the last chapter that you keep a database of your Linkedin connections.

While this process is extra work for you, there is value in saving your contact list on a regular basis. At any time you could run amok of your Linkedin Terms of Service and lose access to your contacts.

Backing up your list won't provide you with the rich content you can discover about a connection however, you will at least have their contact info.

You can export a list of the connections you have made on LinkedIn at any time.

From LinkedIn:

To export LinkedIn connections:

CLICK THE ME ICON AT THE TOP OF YOUR LINKEDIN HOMEPAGE.

Select **Settings & Privacy** from the dropdown.

Click the **Privacy** tab at the top of the page.

Under the **How LinkedIn uses your data section**, click **Change** next to **Download your data.**

Note: You may be prompted to sign in.

You'll be redirected to the **Download your data page** where you can select **Connections.**

You will receive an email to your Primary Email address which will include a link where you can download your list of connections.

The CSV and vCard formats don't support all characters. As a result, languages with extended character sets, such as Chinese, Japanese, or Hebrew are not supported.

You currently can't export a list of your contacts that are not 1st-degree connections.

If you're exporting your connections because you have a duplicate account, remember to:

Close your extra account.

Import your connections list to another LinkedIn account, make sure you've saved the file in a location you can find, and then follow the instructions for uploading contacts using a CSV file.

When you receive your e-mail from Linkedin, you can download it to your computer and then open it with Excel. The downside is only the **full name, email address, current employer, and position** are exported.

You will need to manually access each of your contact's profiles on Linkedin to see if their phone number or mailing address is posted. If so, with a lot of work, you can easily collect the data and add it to your new contact spreadsheet. Be sure to save the spreadsheet with a name you will easily recognize. I change the date on my spreadsheets every time I update so I always have a backup copy should something happen to the one I am currently working on.

33. SYSTEMIZE RESPONDING TO NEW CONNECTIONS

As you build your database of contacts, it is worthwhile sending the new contact a brief message outlining who you are, what you are up to right now and open the door for future possibilities which would include meeting in person.

It has been my experience very few people actually do so. And by doing so, you will stand out from the crowd. For a shy networker this can have the advantage of promoting yourself without increasing your anxiety level.

A few years back I was the Chair of a local entrepreneur's society. I also cared for their social media presence with Facebook and a Linkedin groups. My goal at the time was to be one of the most connected people to the local business world.

As Linkedin members would ask to join the society's Linkedin group, I would assess their suitability for the group and I would also send them back an invitation to join my business and professional network on Linkedin and in the real world.

Utilizing an invitation to connect template i.e. a letter I had created and saved, I sent it out to over 800 Linkedin members who were local business professionals and might be interested in what I had to offer.

As for people I meet at local networking events, if there is a common interest or bond, I will usually connect with them over the next few days. For these individuals I likely wouldn't send them the template message I mentioned above.

If I have met with someone already or had business dealings with them, I would likely adapt the text on the template to refer to our experience together and target what I am promoting to their interests.

34. PARTICIPATE IN LINKEDIN GROUPS

Linkedin Groups provide a place for professionals in the same industry or with similar interests to share content, find answers, post and view jobs, make business contacts, and establish themselves as industry experts. Joining a group is a good way to increase your network of connections. Some groups are private to the members only, so only the members would see your posts. Other groups that are public would allow your posts to be seen by anyone.

You can find groups to join in the **Groups Directory** or view suggestions of groups you may like. You can also create a new group focused on a particular topic or industry.

Finding a group you want to join:

1. Move your cursor over **Groups** at the top of your homepage and select **Groups Directory** from the dropdown menu.
2. Browse the **Featured Groups** on the page.
3. Search for a group using the **Search Groups** box on the left.
4. Move your cursor over **Groups** at the top of your homepage and select **Groups You May Like** from the dropdown menu.
5. Browse through their list of suggested groups.

Choosing the right group for you:

You can get more details about a group and find out if people in your network are members on the **Group Profile** page.

1. Click a group's name to view its **Discussions** page.
2. Click the **More...** tab under the group's name and select **Group Profile.**

Joining a group:

- Click **Join Group** on the group **Discussions** page or anywhere you see the button.

OR

- Respond to an invitation from a group member or manager.

SOMETHING TO KEEP IN MIND IS THERE ARE TWO KINDS OF GROUPS: closed and open. When you post to an open group, your comments will appear in the Updates section for all of your connections to view. If this is desirable, then this works for you. If you are posting something you assumed was private or confidential to a specific group, it may be problematic. Rule of thumb is to not post anything that could come back to haunt you.

If you don't see a group that meets your needs, consider creating your own. You can belong to up to 50 groups and own 10.

I am the Owner of a Linkedin group for a non-profit society for entrepreneurs that I was also the Chairman of the Board. The group is closed to members and you have to ask to join it. I try to limit membership to local business people, entrepreneurs and professionals. As this is my target market for my business as well, it serves as a source of new connections for me.

35. BLOW YOUR OWN HORN

I've mentioned it a few times already in this book. To be successful in business, you need to be able to self-promote... blow your own horn so to speak. The same applies in being a successful networker. If you are researching others, likely they are researching you as well. Make sure you give them something to remember you by.

If you are providing a service or a product that others do as well, you will need to try to stand out from the crowd. Linkedin Basic includes **Slide Share** which allows you to upload a Powerpoint Presentation to www.slideshare.net and have it be accessible on your Profile. It can be a great way to promote yourself and your product or service.

The **newsfeed** section of your profile gives you up-to-date notifications from those you are connected to. Ask a question, share a thought or post an article. This feature can be a good way to send out announcements about special projects you are involved with or to promote something of importance to you. If you have a blog and you have just released the latest edition, promote it here. While it is possible to do, resist the urge to have your Facebook and Twitter account automatically post your content to Linkedin. Each of these three social media venues has their advantages but what works in one might not in the other.

The **newsfeed** is also a great way to keep tabs on the interests of people you may be considering networking with. With each post you have the opportunity to <u>Like</u>, <u>Share</u> or <u>Comment</u>. This can be a good way to start an on-line relationship. It can make it easier for you if and when you actually meet this connection in person. You will already have something in common and can build on it from there.

Sharing your accomplishments will help you find opportunities to teach others, which is part of the process of networking. Be proud of all your accomplishments, whether they seem small, large, significant, easy or difficult. Allow your natural talents & abilities to be the gift you give to your network.

The concept of 'blowing your own horn' may be difficult for some people. Many of us have been taught that talking about yourself is bragging. I believe that it was Walt Whitman who said "If you done it, it ain't bragging!" A technique that works well at removing that illusion of bragging is to submit an update that focuses on someone else.

An example could be "I would like to thank XXX for inviting me to speak at their recent conference on my favourite topic of Conflict Resolution!"

If XXX is a member of Linkedin, the message will show up on their Updates as well as yours. So on one hand you are thanking the other person who will likely appreciate being recognized publicly, but it will also draw attention to your name and whatever you are trying to draw attention to. In this example, I am focusing on speaking about conflict resolution. This falls into a 'win-win' situation and would increase the likelihood might research the fact I present seminars on conflict resolution.

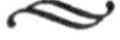

36. STRATEGIC PLANNING:

Over the next few chapters we dive into how to develop your emcee business, starting with creating your business plan.

$\sim$

The first stage in any business project development is that of planning. This stage can save you a lot of time, energy and money down the road, if you give the process the care and consideration it needs.

Benjamin Franklin is often quoted as saying 'If you fail to plan, you are planning to fail!' I wasn't there when he said it, so I don't know if he was referring to business planning, but it seems to apply.

While many call the Business Plan a document, it is more aptly described as a series of processes. In many cases the purpose of a business plan is to secure financing. If you aren't looking for finances, the business plan can help you to organize.

$\sim$

The business plan will be dynamic, in that it will change as you move forward with the development of your business. In the beginning, it serves as a tool to help you make critical decisions. Your business plan is a *strategic* plan.

When you are focusing on your current project i.e. working as an Emcee, it can be easy to lose sight of the big picture. That's why a business review or preparation of a strategic plan is a virtual necessity. This may not be a recipe for success, but without it a business is much more likely to fail.

A sound plan should:

• Serve as a framework for decisions or for securing support/approval.

• Provide a basis for a more detailed planning.

• Explain the business to others in order to inform, motivate & involve.

• Assist benchmarking & performance monitoring.

• Stimulate change and become a building block for the next plan.

I just mentioned that a business plan is a *strategic* plan. This can be a little confusing in that a **Strategic Plan** is an entity in its own right and should not be confused with a business plan.

The former is likely to be a (very) short document whereas a business plan is usually a much more substantial and detailed document. A *strategic plan* can provide the foundation and frame work for a business plan.

Let's address the **Strategic Plan** first and get it out of the way so we can focus on our Business Plan.

The Strategic Plan, at its essence, provides a basis for more detailed planning. It allows you to explain your business to others in order to inform, motivate and involve.

A *strategic plan* is not the same as an *operational plan*. The former should be visionary, conceptual and directional in contrast to an operational plan which is likely to be shorter term, tactical, focused, implementable and measurable.

As an example, compare the process of planning a vacation (where, when, duration, budget, who goes, how you will travel... are all strategic issues) with the final preparations (tasks, deadlines, funding, weather, packing, transport and so on are all operational matters).

A satisfactory *strategic plan* must be realistic and attainable to allow you to think strategically and act operationally.

Well, that's enough talk *about* a strategic plan, this isn't intended to be a business administration course. Let's look now at how to *create* one.

One useful technique for developing your strategic plan is to free-associate a little... to let your mind roam, exploring every avenue you'd like your business to go down. Try writing a personal essay on your business goals. It could take the form of a letter to yourself, written from five years in the future, describing all you have accomplished and how it came about.

In creating your Strategic Plan, you should be determining your 'why.'

Why do you want to run an emcee business? What is driving you? Is it strictly for the money, or are you passionate about it? Both are good reasons.

As you create your document, you may make a surprising discovery, such as you don't really want to own a large, fast-growing enterprise but would be content with a stable small business. Even if you don't learn anything new, though, getting a firm handle on your goals and objectives is a big help in deciding how you'll plan your business.

If you're having trouble, deciding what your goals and objectives are, here are some questions to ask yourself:

- As mentioned earlier, what is the goal of your business

- How determined am I to see this succeed?
- What is my budget? Can I afford to do this right?
- Am I willing to invest my own money and work long hours for no pay, sacrificing personal time and lifestyle, maybe for years?
- What's going to happen to me if this venture doesn't work out?
- Who is my target audience? Will it be a niche market, or will I sell a broad spectrum of good and services?
- What is the profile of my ideal client?
- Do I plan to do all the work myself, do a portion of the work myself, or pay someone to do all the work?
- What will be its annual revenues in a year? Five years?
- What will be its market share in that time frame?

ONCE YOU COMPLETE THE ABOVE QUESTIONNAIRE ASSESSING YOUR GOALS and objectives, here's another strategic assessment tool that is valuable in the planning stage of your business venture.

AN EFFECTIVE STRATEGIC PLANNING TOOL FOR ANY BUSINESS VENTURE IS the **SWOT Analysis.**

From Wikipedia:

SWOT analysis (or SWOT matrix) is a strategic planning technique used to help a person or organization Identify the *Strengths, Weaknesses, Opportunities, and Threats* related to business competition or project planning.

It is intended to specify the objectives of the business venture or project and identify the internal and external factors that are favorable and unfavorable to achieving those objectives.

Users of a SWOT analysis often ask and answer questions to generate meaningful information for each category to make the tool useful and identify their competitive advantage.

Strengths and Weakness are frequently *internally related*, while Opportunities and Threats commonly focus on *environmental placement*.

● **Strengths:** characteristics of the business or project that give it an advantage over others.

● **Weaknesses:** characteristics of the business that place the business or project at a disadvantage relative to others.

● **Opportunities:** elements in the environment that the business or project could exploit to its advantage.

● **Threats:** elements in the environment that could cause trouble for the business or project.

WHAT MAKES SWOT PARTICULARLY POWERFUL IS THAT, WITH A LITTLE thought, it can help you uncover opportunities you are well-placed to exploit. And by understanding the weaknesses of your business, you can manage and eliminate threats that would otherwise catch you unawares.

It can be particularly helpful in making your 'go' 'no go' decision about starting your business or whether you should look in other directions.

Strengths and weaknesses are often *internal* to your business, while opportunities and threats generally relate to *external* factors.

Let's break it down to its individual steps.

Strengths:

- What advantages do you have over other emcees?
- What do you do better than anyone else?

- What skills do you have that would add to your business venture?
- What unique or lowest-cost resources can you draw upon that others can't?
- If considering starting an Emcee business, what experience do you have? [may be a strength or a weakness]
- What do people in your market see as your strengths? [assumes you are already in the market]
- What factors need to be in place for you to "get the sale?"
- What is your Unique Selling Proposition (USP)?

IF YOU'RE HAVING DIFFICULTY GENERATING A LIST OF YOUR STRENGTHS, it can be helpful to use the brain-storming technique.

Don't limit yourself to generating business related strengths. Just list all of your strengths. You may find that a seemingly nonbusiness related skill may be transferable to your business strengths list. Having strong people skills comes to mind.

We tend to be more attuned to our weaknesses or perceived short-comings than we are to our strengths. Don't be too brutal on your self when completing your Weaknesses List.

Weaknesses:

- What skills do you need in this business venture to be successful but don't currently possess?
- How are your technology skills?
- What *could* you improve?
- What *should* you avoid?
- How are your time-management skills or organizational skills?
- What are people in your market likely to see as weaknesses?
- What factors could lose sales?

AGAIN, CONSIDER THIS FROM AN INTERNAL AND EXTERNAL PERSPECTIVE: do other people seem to perceive weaknesses you don't see? Are your competitors doing any better than you?

Opportunities:

- What good opportunities can you spot?
- What interesting trends are you aware of?
- Useful opportunities can come from such things as:
- Changes in technology and markets on both a broad and narrow scale.
- Changes in government policy related to your field.
- Changes in social patterns, population profiles, lifestyle changes, and so on.
- Local events.

A useful approach when looking at opportunities is to look at your strengths and ask yourself whether these open up any opportunities. Alternatively, look at your weaknesses and ask yourself whether you could open up opportunities by eliminating them or turning them into strengths.

Threats:

- What obstacles do you face?
- Do you have the time to take on this venture? [some people are calling this 'bandwidth']
- What are your competitors doing?
- Is the market saturated for your emcee business idea?
- Are quality standards or specifications for your products or services changing?
- Is changing technology threatening your position?
- Do you have bad debt or cash-flow problems?

- Could any of your weaknesses seriously threaten your business?
- Have you had a bad public relations experience in the past that may still be on-line to haunt you?

When I completed the Threat portion of my SWOT analysis for my Mr. Emcee business in relation to taking on wedding reception emcee opportunities, I found my biggest competition was from local deejays.

In addition to providing music and entertainment for wedding receptions, they were offering emcee services for the reception as well. From the client's perspective, they see this as being better value in hiring one person, rather than two.

SO NOW WHAT?

You have completed your SWOT, so what do you do with the information you have learned about yourself and your business idea?

One way of using SWOT is matching and converting. Matching is used to find a competitive advantage by matching the strengths to opportunities.

Another tactic is to convert weaknesses or threats into strengths or opportunities. An example of a conversion strategy is to find new markets.

If the threats or weaknesses cannot be converted, a business should try to minimize or avoid them.

LOGISTICS & ACTION PLAN STEPS:

1. Start developing your Emcee business plan.

2. Prepare a short strategic plan.

3. Is your strategic plan realistic and attainable?

4. Does your strategic plan address your 'why'?

5. Have you answered the questions identified in the creating your Strategic Plan segment offered in this chapter?

6. Were there any surprises revealed or problems identified?

7. Complete a SWOT analysis focusing on the services you plan to offer.

37. CREATING YOUR BUSINESS PLAN: OVERVIEW

As we've discussed in the previous chapter on strategic planning, your strategic planning leads into the development of your more formalized Business Plan.

We went into creating your elevator pitch earlier in this book as part of marketing strategies, however this is a good time to create one as part of your business plan.

Craft a rough pitch for your business. Use a hundred words or so to explain what your business is about, who it is for, how it is unique in comparison to all the others who provide emcee services and what the client will gain by engaging you.

It can be a challenge to cover in a hundred words or so. Give it a try.

HERE'S A QUICK OVERVIEW OF WHAT YOU CAN GENERALLY EXPECT IN A business plan. As an emcee, your version may or may not include all the categories suggested.

1. **Executive Summary:** Write this last. It's just a page or two of highlights.

2. **Company Description:** Legal establishment, history, start-up plans etc.

3. **Production or Service:** Describe what you're selling. Focus on customer benefits.

4. **Market Analysis:** You need to know your market, customer needs, where they are, how to reach them, etc.

5. **Strategy & Implementation:** Be specific. Include management responsibilities i.e. yours, with dates and budgets. Make sure you can track results.

6. **Financial Analysis:** Make sure to include at the very least your projected Profit & Loss and Cash Flow Tables.

～

Start your business plan with a quick assessment. For a first look, consider your objectives, mission statement and keys to success.

Objectives: Objectives are business goals. Set your market share objectives, sales objectives, and profit objectives. Businesses need to set objectives and plan to achieve them.

Make sure your objectives are concrete and measurable.

Mission Statement: Use the mission statement to define your business concept. A business mission statement should define underlying goals (such as making a profit) and objectives in broad strategic terms, including what market is served and what benefits are offered.

For illustrative purposes, we will be looking at developing your business plan with the idea that you will be developing an Emcee business.

～

An important part of your business plan is the *MARKET ANALYSIS*:

- Who is your ideal client?

- Demographics? [statistical data relating to the population and particular groups within it.]

- How big is the market?

- How much money do people spend?

- What are the numbers?

In the process of analyzing the market, you are looking at how to improve things.

What are *your* market needs?

Then there is the ***competitive analysis***. For you to be competitive in the marketplace, you need to understand what the competition has to offer.

Look at the providers of services similar to yours.

We look at conducting your **Competitive Analysis** in greater detail in the next chapter.

Business plans are dynamic. They are a creative process. After going through your plan two or three times, you will get a better idea of what is missing.

Another step in the business plan is the ***Promotion Plan***. How will you market and promote your business? Will you have enough money to afford to promote your business?

Your promotion plan should include building your business website. Are you able to do it yourself or will you need to pay someone to develop it for you?

Some entrepreneurs believe in creating a mission statement for the business plan where they outline what they want to accomplish. What benefits do I need to provide my clients? What promises do I want to make to the client I want to fulfill?

Still working our way through the steps of developing your business plan, you will need to look at financial considerations. Are there people you need to hire to take your business to the next level? This may include an accountant, lawyer etc.

Then create a budget to cover those expenses. A profit-loss statement, even if it is based on guestimation, can give you an idea of what you need to be profitable. This will come into play when you determine the price you want to charge for your services and what the market will bear.

Before you even start your business, think about the big picture. Think about your future. Plot your ten-year course. The different steps in your business plan allows you to plot your course.

As mentioned earlier, your business plan is dynamic. It isn't designed to be created, read a couple times and then filed away in your computer. It is meant to be used on a regular basis. In upcoming chapters, we explore how to use your business plan as a tool to monitor your success in business.

Your business plan will help in keeping track of your expenses and sales.

In the next few chapters, we explore some essential elements of your business plan in greater detail.

～

38. CONDUCTING A COMPETITIVE ANALYSIS

Conducting a competitive analysis

Let's dive a little deeper into the *Competitive Analysis* portion of our business plan.

Overview:

The Competitive Analysis is a statement of the business strategy and how it relates to the competition. The purpose of the competitive analysis is to determine the strengths and weaknesses of the competitors within your market space, assist you to develop strategies that will provide you with a distinct advantage over your competition, the barriers that can be developed in order to prevent competition from entering your market, and any weaknesses that can be exploited within the product development cycle.

If you ignore or minimize the impact competition will have on your business prospects, then you have an unrealistic business plan.

If you were creating your business plan for the purpose of obtaining funding, as you would in many businesses, investors and other readers of your business plan will expect you have completed your due diligence.

The competitive analysis section can be the most difficult section to compile when writing a business plan. Before you can analyze your competitors, you have to investigate them.

Gathering Information on Competitors: First, Find Out Who They Are

The first step of preparing your competitive analysis is to determine who your current and potential competitors are. Identifying all existing and potential sources of competition is an impossible task, indirect and future competitors can number in the tens, hundreds, or even thousands. Instead, you will have to draw the line somewhere when it comes to identifying major competitors -- the ones that are going to have a real impact on your business over time.

There are essentially two ways you can identify competitors. The first is to look at the market from the customer's viewpoint and group all your competitors by the degree to which they contend for the buyer's dollar.

The second method is to group competitors according to their various competitive strategies, so you understand what motivates them.

HERE IS A QUICK OVERVIEW OF WHAT YOU NEED TO KNOW ABOUT YOUR competition:

- Who is your competition?
- What markets or market segments do your competitors serve?
- What benefits does your competition offer?
- Why do customers buy from them?
- What strategies are your competitors pursuing and how successful are these strategies? i.e. What are my competitors doing that I can learn from?
- What are their strengths and weaknesses?

- What could I do better?
- How can I present similar products or services in a distinctive manner?
- What section of the market (if any) are they not capturing?
- How are they marketing themselves?
- What threats do they pose?
- How are my competitors likely to respond to any changes to the way I do business?

In his book [Even More Offensive Marketing], Hugh Davidson likens the process of gathering competitive data to a jigsaw puzzle. Each individual piece of data does not have much value.

The important skill is to collect as many of the pieces as possible and to assemble them into an overall picture of the competitor. This enables you to identify any missing pieces and to take the necessary steps to collect them.

We could go into a lot deeper detail on this subject of creating your competitive analysis, however I think we are starting to get beyond the scope of this book.

There is an inexpensive software package I have used a couple times and would recommend, *BusinessPlan Maker Professional* from Individual Software. When using the software, the information you have gathered and analyzed will help you complete the *Industry, Competition & Market section* of your business plan.

39. FINANCIAL PLANNING

As in any business venture, considering financial matters is a necessity and is a crucial component of your Emcee's Business Plan.

As you work your way through the planning process, you will be called on to take your best guess regarding the key operational issues facing your business. You'll have to make estimates regarding productivity, capacity, cash flow, costs, and many other interrelated factors.

If you aren't a numbers person, you may be tempted to avoid this section and 'wing' it. That would be ill advised. It might be helpful to find someone who is good with numbers to help you out. Even if it costs you some money for their time, it could be an investment that saves you a lot of money in the long term.

How do you plan on paying for the development costs for your business? Have you given any thoughts to the expenses you will incur? What will you charge for your service? How much are similar emcees charging for their services in the marketplace? Are they providing anything different from you are?

From a practical standpoint, there are two potential sources for the information you need to make reasonable assumptions. If you have an existing business, you have your personal experiences on which to rely.

Even if you're taking on a new product or trying to enter a new market, your experience in the industry in general will serve you well.

The same holds true if you have experience in your industry, but not as a business owner. Many new businesses are started by people who have experience as an employee in the same or a related field. If that applies to you, what you learned will serve you well as you strike out on your own.

While there is no substitute for personal experience, you can derive a large benefit by drawing on the experiences of those around you. Unless you're starting a completely new type of business, there will be someone around with experience at what you're planning to do. You'd be surprised how willing even potential competitors are to share information, if asked in the right way. This is particularly true if your business will serve a limited geographic market and won't directly compete with a similar business located some distance away.

- MARKETING & PROMOTION

- Website developing, maintenance & hosting

As a business owner, with the intent of making revenue, as compared to an emcee who emcees as a hobby, you are entitled to claim home office expenses on your income tax claim. These expenses may include a computer, computer software purchased for your business, office furniture, stationary, etc.

If you have your home office already set up, it can be a fairly simple process of importing the information into your business plan as Owner's Assets brought into the business.

If you need to purchase your office equipment, you will have to factor those expenses into your start-up expenses on your financial balance sheet as part of your business plan.

As part of your financial planning, you will need to determine the price of your service. What will the market bear? How many gigs can you expect to provide?

This is an area that you will most likely guestimate.

It can be helpful to do a break-even analysis at this point. By totalling the costs of all your expense estimates and dividing it by the price that you have settled upon, you will learn the number of bookings you need to complete to break even.

After completing a break-even analysis, you may be faced with a difficult decision. If the cost of production looks to be too high and your return on investment too low, is it even worth going into business or completing this business plan at all?

If so, might there be some changes you can make to your business plan to make it a viable business venture? Perhaps spending some money on developing your skills could save you money by taking on some necessary tasks yourself, instead of having to pay others to do them.

THROUGH THE LAST FEW CHAPTERS WE HAVE BEEN LOOKING AT strategizing and developing several plans essential to the success of starting your business.

In the next chapter we look at deciding what entity your author or self-publishing business should take on.

40. CHOOSING YOUR BUSINESS ENTITY

As an entrepreneur, going into business for yourself, one of the first decisions you need to make is what form of entity your business will take.

The pros and cons of different business formations are worth understanding. They vary by state and country, so this isn't a good area for guesswork. I'm going to provide you with a brief overview of what is available. I'm not a lawyer and they are the people to approach for information and advice, specific to your needs.

Although details vary, it starts with the choice between a sole proprietorship, partnership, corporation and Limited Liability Company (LLC) [where available].

The simplest form is the sole proprietorship. Simply put, your business is a sole proprietorship if you don't create a separate legal entity for it. This is true whether you operate it in your own name, or under a trade name. If it isn't your own name, then you register your business name as a "Fictitious Business Name" or a DBA ("Doing Business As")

Different geographical regions, depending on where you live, may have on-line websites where you can register your business name for a nominal fee. This may give you some protection in the case of somebody else wanting to use the business name you have chosen. In addition to the application completion, some regions may require you to place an announcement in your local newspaper or perhaps a trade journal, announcing the fact that you are doing business as...

You are best to spend some time on the internet researching to ensure there isn't a business locally that already has the name you are thinking of using. Hopefully, there isn't. Neither do you want to choose a name close to another's business name as it may be confusing to customers and cause you problems sometime in the future.

When I registered two business names over the past few years, the on-line registration system advised me to choose up to three different business names, just in case one or two of them are not accepted. This was done on the same application process.

It might be different in your area, but it would be a good idea to develop several names just in case. It could save you some money.

Sole Proprietorship:

The main disadvantage of the sole proprietorship is the lack of a separate entity, which means you have a personal responsibility for it. If your business fails, then your creditors can go after your personal assets.

Tax treatment is quite simple, your business profit and loss goes straight through to your personal taxes. This can be good or bad for your tax situation, depending on where you stand with other income.

Partnerships:

Partnerships can be challenging to describe as the terms may be very different in various geographical regions.

At the basic level, a partnership agreement outlines the agreed upon terms among the partners. The agreements can define different levels of risk, which is why you often read about partnerships that have general partners and limited partners, with different levels of risk for each. Usually, the income or loss from the partnership passes through to the partners, without any partnership tax. The agreement usually defines what happens if a partner withdraws, buy and sell arrangements for partners, and liquidation arrangements should it become necessary.

Thinking of liquidating your business when you are setting it up, seems a lot like planning for your divorce, while you are standing at the altar. Nevertheless, situations do occur where a little pre-planning could have prevented major headaches down the road. I have personally heard of situations where one of the partners has died, leaving their share of the business to their wife. Unfortunately, the wife had no interest in being involved in the business. This resulted in the surviving partner having to buy out the grieving widow, even though they weren't in a position to do so.

A few years back, I was cowriting and publishing a book with a colleague and considering creating a partnership. I sought out legal-council and was advised not to consider a partnership. One of the big deal-breaking clauses would have been that my partner in the agreement could take on major debt on behalf of the partnership, without my knowledge and leave me responsible to pay it back. That could mean that I could end up losing my house, if my partner were to become unscrupulous. That was way too much risk for the co-publishing of a simple book. We never did publish the book.

Incorporation:

Incorporation is the formation of a new corporation (a corporation being a legal entity that is effectively recognized as a person under the law). The corporation may be a business, a nonprofit organization, sports club, or a government of a new city or town. (from Wikipedia)

The decision to incorporate is not one that should be taken lightly or made on a whim. There are advantages to incorporating, but there are also drawbacks.

Some advantages being it secures your assets and can gain tax breaks. Corporation owners enjoy limited liability protection and are typically not personally responsible for business debts. Another plus: corporations often gain tax advantages, writing off such things as health insurance premiums, savings on self-employment taxes, and life insurance.

A colleague of mine incorporated her self-publishing business she had created to self-publish her book. After two years of having to complete onerous and expensive tax preparation, she decided to close down the corporation and revert to a sole proprietor. The costs and effort of maintaining the corporation, far outweighed her book sales.

If you are unsure whether you should or how to incorporate, you should talk with both legal and tax professionals to determine if incorporating is the right move for you and your business.

LLC (Limited Liability Company)

This business entity can differ from state to state and isn't available in all countries. It apparently can be more difficult to set up than a corporation.

In general, the LLC has to be missing two of the four characteristics of a corporation (limited liability, centralized management, continuity of life and free transferability of ownership interest.) Confused? I am!

I'm not sure why you would want to set up your business this way but it is an entity that needs mentioning.

41. EMCEE OPPORTUNITIES

I f you live in a larger community, meetings of all sizes… from conferences to annual general meetings to conventions are taking place regularly.

From my perspective, challenges that Emcees often face is event organizers, whether they be independent or in-house, are not aware the value a professional Emcee can bring to their event, or are under the belief that anybody can do it and they will do it for free.

Here are some opportunities for Emcees that come to mind:

- Chamber of Commerce annual business awards events
- Local business associations annual business awards events
- Nonprofit [not for profit] organizations annual recognition events
- Professional associations general meetings
- Educational organizations professional development events
- Corporate organizations professional development events
- Private industry professional development events
- Wedding receptions
- Celebrations of Life

- Life celebrations e.g. birthdays, retirement, farewell celebrations
- School graduation ceremonies
- Charitable fund raiser events
- Charity fundraising auctions
- Sports banquets e.g. golf, bowling, darts, etc.
- New product or service awareness events
- Public political candidate forums/debates
- Media [press] conferences
- Public Townhall forums

42. MODERATING A PANEL DISCUSSION

Panel discussions have become a feature of many conference and convention agendas and it's often the role of the Emcee to moderate or facilitate the discussion. They may also be organized as a community-based stand-alone event.

A panel discussion is a method of informing a group about a subject or exploring a subject in greater depth and is presented by a smaller group. This small group, or panel, is generally made up of people who have knowledge and experience about the subject under discussion and are able to speak on the topic with some authority.

A panel discussion adds variety to a program and can add a more comprehensive perspective than a single presenter can. A panel of four speakers can each provide a different perspective to a topic. They don't necessarily even have to agree with each other. Disagreement can add excitement and interest to an otherwise dry topic.

As the Emcee or Moderator of a panel discussion your event organizer may have already completed all the organization steps i.e. deciding on the topic, choosing the panellists, creating the questions. Perhaps not! It may become your responsibility to take on any or all of the logistical requirements of pulling it together.

Thinking logistically, here is the sequence of steps you need to take to ensure the success of your panel discussion.

Define the Problem that will be discussed.

Your first task is to narrow the problem or question that is for discussion. You have a limited amount of time for the activity and narrowing the focus of the topic so it can be adequately covered in the given amount of time can be very challenging. At the same time you need to create a topic that is not only of interest to your target audience but it has to engage them.

Three categories can be used to determine the problem to be discussed:

Problems of Fact refer to questions of truth and falsity. The kinds of information you will consider are factual statements that can be verified and tested. Proven facts, including statistics, provide good supporting material in arriving to a conclusion. "What manner of development will generate more tax revenue for the local community?" is an example of a problem of fact.

As the Moderator you will need to remember to interpret and clarify facts so the group reaches a common understanding. If you choose to discuss a question of fact, you may be able to correct errors or misperceptions held by audience members.

Problems of Value concern the attitudes you hold and the judgements you make. Discussions of questions of value rely on facts to support the position you may take toward solving a particular problem. "In terms of environmental impact, is it more beneficial to develop the land as a park and natural wildlife refuge?" is a question of value.

Problems of Policy require you decide what procedure to use or what action to take to achieve some goal. Given this kind of problem, you and your group will encounter wide points of view in considering alternative choices.

Selecting the Panellists

Looking at the scope and the importance of the problem to be discussed, you will need to secure up to four individuals who are knowledgeable about the subject and are capable of speaking comfortably before a group.

Outlining the Points to Be Covered

You will need to select the panellists on the basis of their knowledge and expertise, which allows for a division of the subject according to their corresponding fields of authority. You will also need to discuss with each individual the nature of the information to be presented and insure each knows what the others will cover.

An example of a panel discussion I organized was based on the overall theme of raising awareness for elder abuse prevention. Throughout the forum speakers presented topics related to financial and/or sexual abuse of the elderly, community & government funded resources for seniors, police resources and abuse prevention. Four of the speakers were invited to participate in a panel discussion on how to raise awareness of the topic.

Moderating the Discussion

You will need to determine where and how you want your panellists to be seated. Options include sitting on chairs, behind a table at the front of the room. Other options are seated on chairs without a table or perhaps perched on stools, at the front of the room. Your panellist's comfort should be considered. If you will be using stools you may want to caution female panellists about wearing **dresses** or skirts as it may cause some discomfort for them and draw the audience's attention to something they may not appreciate.

If you are using a head table and chairs format, consider using tent style name placards to help the audience track who each speaker is.

There are at least two different approaches to introducing your panellists. One is to introduce all of the speakers, individually, in order of where they are seated. You should start off by introducing each panellist and their topic for presentation. Your introductions should be brief but cover the necessary information of the speaker's name, why they are qualified to talk on this particular topic and what they will be talking about.

A second method is to introduce each speaker as it is their turn to present. I'm in favour of giving a brief introduction of the panellists, in turn, then a slightly longer one that also introduces their topic, when they are ready to present.

After the panellists have spoken, your task is to present a summary of the points discussed and conclusions offered. This is not the time to interject your personal views on the subject. Your role is to remain neutral. Having said that, I realize there have been many times where I have personally broken that advice. It can easily happen that the panel discussion has been lacklustre and in need of an interjection to resuscitate it.

Question and Answer Session

Your audience likely has questions. You can either allow questions to be posed as the discussion progresses or wait until the end of all the panellist's presentations. There are advantages and disadvantages to each way.

As an Emcee I'm in favour of allowing questions to be posed after each segment or each panellist has made their presentation. It allows the audience to stay focused on the topic at hand, allowing them to follow the flow of the discussion easier. You need to be skilful in handling questions in this format in that a question can easily be off the main topic or sidetrack it i.e. in a direction it shouldn't be going.

If it has been a stand and deliver style of a panel discussion with questions being allowed at the end, audience members may be keeping their question in their mind for some time. This can prevent their focus on the current discussion and increase their anxiety level if they feel passionate about the topic and their question.

Handling question-and-answer sessions is a skill every Emcee should develop. Often an audience member's question isn't a question at all, perhaps more of a statement. It can be a thinly veiled attempt to set the questioner up as an expert on the subject with the purpose of drawing attention to themselves or discrediting any or all of the panellists.

It can help to request this individual to clarify what their actual question is so it can be considered by the panel. This can have the result of disempowering the questioner who is likely looking for attention and their own audience.

Other Logistics to Consider

Depending on the size of the room you will be using you may need to consider sound amplification i.e. mics and speakers. Using mics you can get away with a minimum of two. One for you as the moderator which is often tethered into a lectern/podium and another wired or wireless that the panellists can share among themselves.

Dominating or Passive Panellists

I have seen both, frequently. An individual who purports to be an accomplished speaker can freeze when the time comes to present or become passive in an open forum Q&A session. Conversely, a panellist may exhibit domineering tendencies where they take more than their share of the time allotted. As the Moderator your task is to ensure all of your panellists have an equitable opportunity.

You may find you have to direct questions to a panellist who is shy and reluctant to jump in and contribute or even put some time sanctions on the overbearing panellist.

I moderated one panel discussion where one of the panellists, who was obviously more experienced on the topic than the others, took over the discussion in a facilitative fashion. As it seemed to be effective and took the discussion in a positive, forward motion, as the Moderator I sat back and let things unfold. When the discussion developed to a strategic point to do so, I took back the role of Moderator and took our discussion to its natural conclusion. There was nothing pre-planned with this occurrence, it just happened. One could call it synergy as it turned into something far better than what was planned.

Timing

As the Moderator it is your role to ensure each panellist as well as you speaks to time. There is only so much time available and you have to continually be aware of the milestones i.e. where you need to be in your program at what specific time. You may have to intervene to speed a speaker up or come to a conclusion. Q&A sessions are notorious for eating up more time than allotted. Start on time and end on time! Your audience will appreciate you for it.

Concluding Your Panel Discussion

All good things come to an end and so must your panel discussion. This is where you will thank your presenters and your audience. Then you will encourage them to enjoy the rest of the conference or to send them safely on their merry way.

TIPS FROM THE PROS:

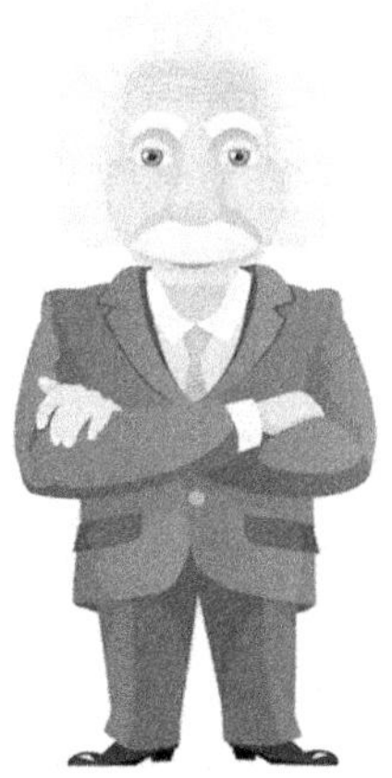

THESE TIPS ARE FROM TIMOTHY HYDE "CORPORATE EMCEE/MC". http://expertmc.com/

- Remember, "It's not about you!" Your role is to encourage the free flowing discussion, but also keeping it on track and importantly on time.
- Make sure the panel knows what time you are going to finish and subtly bring this up at the 5 minute to go mark. I also let the audience know if appropriate.
- Do you really need to go into lengthy introductions? Time zooms by in most Panel discussions, why waste it in lengthy intros?
- A "holding slide" featuring the panel member and their role can work well. Then a slide of all the panel members. (Editorial Note: This tip refers to having a Power Point slide presentation with slides rotating and featuring each of the panellists. Presumably, this would reduce the amount of time that you as the Emcee would have to spend introducing each of the panellists.)
- Get out from behind the Panel Table! A nice array of chairs or stools means a closer connection between the panel members themselves and between them and their audience.
- Mix things up a bit. Why do Q & A at the end?

- Keep the audience involved. Poll them at certain points.
- Create "table discussions" and then get feedback from a few and then ask the panel to comment on that feedback. This process works well if the audience are shy in asking questions. They are usually happy to chat around a table.
- Get Context - If questions or comments are coming from the floor it's nice to know who the person asking the question is and their role. This can provide a context for the panel to answer more appropriately.
- Be prepared to be firm with the audience. If the conversation gets too heated or inappropriate, be prepared to step in and then move on. "I think we can agree to disagree on that." "That is probably beyond the scope of our discussion today." And follow with your own question.
- On the other hand, be prepared to step back when the conversation is lively and free flowing.
- Wrapping Up. It's nice to get a quick comment from each panel member right near the end. Perhaps – Big Challenge for the next year? Action Steps for the audience members, Key Points, etc.
- Being comfortable running sessions in this format is a skill. It's also a good selling point. You add value to the event by being able to run these sessions, so make sure you mention it in your promotional material as a benefit of booking you.

43. SAMPLE EMCEEING CONTRACT

S ample Contract:

If there will be an exchange of money for your serving as an Emcee you should consider having the terms of the event recorded in a contract and signed by you as the Emcee and the event organizer or their agent. Here is a *simple* contract that gives you an idea of some terms that can be used in an emceeing contract.

Disclaimer: This sample contract should be considered as being for illustrative purposes only and you should seek legal advice before using it. The author takes no responsibilities for the outcome of its usage as it is written here and it is provided without warranty.

THIS AGREEMENT IS BETWEEN **XXXXX**, DBA (DOING BUSINESS AS) **ZZZZZ (address) and (Client) (Company) (Address):**

____

DATE OF ENGAGEMENT: ___________________ PROGRAM TIME: ____________

Program Location: _________________________ Program Title:______________

Number of expected participants: _______________

Services Required:

In exchange for the services provided, the Client agrees to compensate XXXXX as follows:

The Business agrees to pay **XXXXX** by Certified Check that is made payable to XXXXX at the conclusion of the presentation. XXXXX shall present, as described herein as an independent contractor, and XXXXX shall have no obligation with regard to such a presentation, as a result of this Agreement to anyone other than the Client.

This constitutes the entire agreement between the parties.

The above information is agreed to and accepted by:

This contract shall be governed by the laws of the State/Province of _________ in _________ County and any applicable Federal Law.

___________________________ Date___________

Signature of the Speaker

___________________________ Date___________

Signature of the Business

44. IT'S SHOWTIME!

S tart on time and end on time.

One of the biggest worries for Event Planners is that the event starts on time and ends on time. If you as the Emcee can ensure both happen at your event, you will be very appreciated by your Event Planner. This can go a long way in increasing the chances you will be asked to officiate at another event.

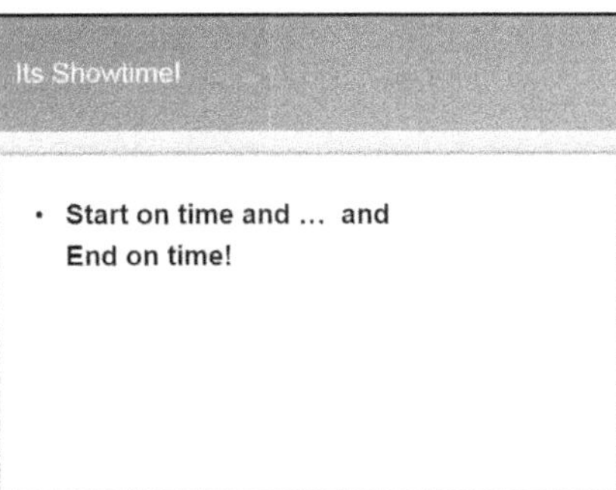

PART III

ADDITIONAL RESOURCES:

Here is a compilation of questions I have answered on quora.com on the subject of emceeing, event organizing and public speaking that may resonate with you.

Some answers were crafted at the time to promote my products or services so I will apologize in advance.

45. QUESTION: MASTER OF CEREMONIES: WHAT IS THE BEST WAY FOR AN MC TO MAKE A NOISY CROWD GO QUIET?

Answer provided...

Trying to get your audience to quieten and focus on what you have to say can be one of the most challenging tasks an emcee has. After all, how can you do your job, if nobody listens to you.

I believe part of the solution is that when you stand behind the mic, take on a persona of being in control. You should be dressed for the part. Many people will naturally look to you to see and hear what you have to say. Odds are, the people in the front will notice you and quiet down accordingly.

But not so those in the back of the room.

You could yell in the mic 'hey you in the back! Shut up, I'm trying to talk here!' As offensive as that sounds, it might work in some circumstances.

Here are some techniques I have seen used.

- Slowly and rhythmically clap your hands into the mic. The people in front will follow along and hopefully the others will follow.

- Slowly and increasingly louder, say 'Can the people in the back hear me? Raise your hand if you can."
- Slowly start counting from one upward. People will get curious to find out why you are counting.
- An air horn can be offensive, yet effective. A blast or two can clear the dust out of the ears of some of your audience members.
- "Raise your hand if you can hear me?" You may have to repeat it a few times until you get their attention.
- "Are you ready to get started!" Repeat, increasingly louder as needed.
- "Are you reaaaady to rumble!! Well we aren't here to rumble but we are here to... so if I can have your attention please."

46. QUESTION: WHAT ARE SOME EMCEE SPEECH EXAMPLES?

A nswer provided...

What are you referring to when you say "EMCEE" speech?

Typically, the Emcee i.e. Master of Ceremonies does not deliver speeches. Their role is to keep the meeting moving smoothly and to introduce the featured speakers.

They are in charge of the show.

Officiating as a Master of Ceremonies at an event is a lot like looking at an iceberg floating in the water. The public only sees what is happening at the event... the tip of the iceberg. They don't see what has happened behind the scenes or under the water, so to speak, to make everything look like it is running smoothly.

47. QUESTION: DO YOU HAVE DIFFICULTY APPLYING A SAFETY FILTER TO YOUR SPEECH AND OVERSHARE PERSONAL INFORMATION?

A nswer provided...

The short answer is "no!"

I believe personal information should be shared in a presentation, within limits.

I listen to speakers because I want to hear their viewpoint on specific subjects, how it has affected them and what they have done about it.

I don't like speeches that come across as canned. Those speeches are packed with fluff, probably somebody else's and don't offer any original thinking or ideas.

While I believe in sharing personal information, I don't believe in TMI [too much information!] That is where the speaker shares personal information that really should be kept private. Perhaps intimate details from a relationship that would be embarrassing to the other party, or to the audience. I'm not sure about a safety filter, but I believe that personal information can be shared within specific parameters. Here are some of them:

- The personal story should have a purpose and add to the speech, not divert from it.
- The personal story should be short and to the point.
- There should be an easily identifiable point. It shouldn't be used as filler to lengthen an otherwise lackluster presentation.
- It should not embarrass anyone in any way.

If your story invokes your emotions, perhaps you aren't ready to share that story yet. You don't want to break down on stage and/or traumatize your audience.

Here's a formula I learned years ago in Toastmasters to create humour out of personal misfortune.

PMF + T=H [personal misfortune + time = humour]

We all have personal misfortunes we have endured and hopefully learned from. These situations become gems for speakers to fit into their speeches. I would recommend speakers reflect upon their life and brainstorm a list of these life-altering experiences. These learning moments can become gems in your presentations.

As an example, I have delivered speeches about bullying bosses. When I was 19 years old, my first job as an adult, I worked in an institutional kitchen and I had a Head Cook who was a bully. We clashed from the get-go.

In one instance he had been riding my case and yelled out to the other cooks "Where's that Stonehouse!" He wasn't aware that I was in earshot. I responded with 'Here I am Dick! Lay a big wet one on me!' And then I promptly lifted my uniform top, bent over and exposed my derrière.

Was it helpful? Certainly not! Was it gratifying? Very much.

As I recall, I got written up again and my punishment was to spend the day in the Bake Shop, cleaning the ovens. It might not have been so bad, if they had turned the ovens off first!

The point: you won't win, when standing up to a serial bully, especially when they have their audience, watching them exert their power. There are other, more effective ways to deal with a workplace bully.

And maybe even more importantly, if you ever get to the point at work that you think about bending over and telling your boss to kiss your ass goodbye... I would suggest rethinking that action, unless you are a motivational speaker looking for real-life stories to share.

48. QUESTION: DISCUSS THE FACTORS TO CONSIDER WHEN PREPARING FOR A SPEECH?

Answer provided…

The initial factors for me depend on whether I have been asked to deliver a speech to a group or whether it is one I have initiated.

Secondly, if I have been asked to speak, do I actually know anything about the subject I am being asked to speak about? Am I the best person to talk on the required topic?

What specifically is the audience looking for? What do they already know? Have they heard from any other speaker on the topic?

If I am qualified and capable to speak on the topic, what's in it for me? It's not always about getting paid for speaking. If I am going to put a significant amount of time into preparing, rehearsing, travelling and delivering, I want something in return. I have learned my time and effort are worth something.

Additional factors I would want to know:

- Age and demographic of the audience?

- How many people will be in the audience [helpful to know for handout preparation]?
- Date, time & location?
- Who will be introducing me?
- Who will be outroducing me? [that's where the person thanks you upon completion of your speech]
- What's happening before and after I am scheduled to speak?
- Will audio-visual equipment be required?
- Will sound amplification be required?
- Are there any taboo subjects?
- If it is a group or organization, has there been any important events happen to them? Examples: a layoff, firings, expansion, mergers and/or deaths

49. QUESTION: IS IT EASY TO MAKE AN INFORMATIVE SPEECH? WHY? WHY NOT?

A nswer provided...

'Easy' is a relative term. What I consider being easy may be considered impossible to another.

There are several elements involved in making an informative speech.

Firstly, you need to have the skills to be able to research your topic. To inform somebody else, you need to be knowledgeable about the subject yourself.

Secondly, you need to be able to filter the content so you deliver the right amount for the time you have and the understanding level of your audience. We are in the information age. There will always be too much information available for any topic.

And thirdly, you need to have the communication and public speaking skills to get your message across effectively.

Other factors come into play such as the topic. A light-hearted topic may be easy to deliver. Whereas a topic such as a public or personal tragedy, may be very difficult to speak about, even if you have good public speaking skills.

50. QUESTION: WHAT IS A VERY GOOD SPEECH ON WHY YOU WANT TO BE A LEADER?

A nswer provided...

THERE LIKELY ISN'T A DEFINITIVE ANSWER TO THIS QUESTION.

The success of your speech depends on its purpose.

Is it for an essay at school? Are you running for an office or political position? Are you looking at being a leader as a career path?

An adage I like to use about leadership is that 'if you think you are leading and nobody is following you... then you are just out for a walk.'

To be a leader, you need to have followers. It isn't a matter of announcing 'hey, I'm your leader, you need to follow me!'

Leadership is demonstrated by your deeds and actions, not your words.

Many so-called leaders have as their root desire, the ability to control people or bend them to their wishes. That is a dictator, not a leader.

While you may have the admiration of your followers and the prestige of being in charge, in your mind, it would be best not to express those thoughts in your speech.

Your speech should be focused on your followers. How do you plan to take them from one place to another? What's in it for them if they follow you? What if they don't?

How do you plan to lead them? What skills, expertise and qualifications do you have to be able to lead? Do you have past leadership experiences to highlight your leadership ability?

Do you have credibility? Do you walk your talk? Many leaders don't.

Do you believe in integrity?

Leadership may have influence at its base. Do you have the communication skills, the self-confidence and the ability to envision a better future and then to lead them there?

These are all elements of a good speech on leadership.

You shouldn't talk about why you want to be a leader. Your speech should be about what you can do to lead others.

You can't push a rope. But you can pull it. Be the type of leader that pulls people where they want to go, not push them there.

If you can do this, you will be an outstanding leader.

51. QUESTION: WHAT DO YOU THINK ABOUT WHEN YOU GIVE A SPEECH?

Answer provided...

There are a myriad of thoughts going through my head when I deliver a speech.

The most obvious of course being the next line I need to deliver. Taking it to a bigger picture I need to think about where the next line is in perspective to the overall story.

Sometimes I need to divert from my script to provide clarity for the audience on an element of the speech or to answer an urgent question. The challenge can be to get back to my original story.

Other thoughts I would put into logistical categories:

Eye Contact: Am I making eye contact with everyone in the audience that I can? Are they returning my eye contact? Do they look like they are understanding my presentation, or do they look puzzled? Does it look like they agree with me or are they disagreeing?

Speed/rate: Am I delivering my presentation at a rate my audience can understand?

Positioning: Am I taking advantage of my speaking area? If I'm videoing my presentation and I am also my own camera operator, am I staying within my camera lens area?

Gestures: Am I using appropriate hand and facial gestures? Are they serving the purpose of what I want them to do i.e. add to my story or are they taking away from it?

Envisioning: While I prepare for my presentation my envisioning my success, I keep those successful thoughts in my mind while I am presenting.

At a different level of consciousness, I am aware of the room temperature and what is going on around the speaking room if it is in a public venue.

52. QUESTION: HOW CAN ONE IMPROVE HIS VOICE IN PRESENTATIONS, AND WHAT ARE THE EXERCISES THAT ENABLE HIM TO MASTER HIS VOICE?

Answer provided...

It would be nice if we could all have access to a voice coach and be able to pay for their services.

Here is some resource material on the subject that will help you work on this challenge yourself. I use it for training purposed in my Toastmasters club. I'm not sure of its original source. Enjoy!

Vocal Variety

Vocal variety is the way you use your voice to create interest, excitement and emotional involvement.

A good voice is:

a. Articulate — clear and distinct

b. Expressive — portrays different shades of meaning

c. Vital — alive and enthusiastic

d. Pleasing — the tone is pleasant to the ear

e. Relaxed — free from tension and affectation

f. Personalized — appropriate to the age, sex and image you desire

Here are four voice variables: pitch, rate, volume and quality. Each is used in varying degrees to add interest to your voice and speech.

Pitch refers to the lowness and the highness of the tone or sound in your voice. The best pitch range is at least 8 notes. A narrow-range bores listeners and they'll quickly "tune out." A good speaker may use as many as 25 different notes to convey variety and meaning.

This is more often a problem for men than for women, because men sometimes (consciously or unconsciously) try not to express too much emotion and, as a result, can sound "flat." Although women generally use more pitch variety, they sometimes get into an upper pitch range, stay there too long and can sound "shrill."

The pitch is too high. Under normal circumstances, this frequently occurs because of nervousness (remember your first talk?), fright or from being overanxious to respond. If you suffer no physical problems that may affect your voice, the more often you speak, the more relaxed your throat muscles will become, resulting in more pleasant vocal sounds.

The pitch is too low. You may know some people who speak with a very low, bass-like sound. Usually they speak slowly. Reading aloud happy, lively material — children's books for example — at a fast pace is a good exercise that may help to raise a low pitch.

To avoid or eliminate a monotone, you must find your normal range. This is the vocal area that is most comfortable for you to carry on a normal conversation and from which you may easily raise or lower your pitch.

Once you establish your normal pitch range, it is crucial to maintain it. Listen to how it sounds and feels when you use it so that whenever you speak, it becomes as natural as breathing.

Inflections comprise another important characteristic of speech. An inflection is a raised pitch — a high note used to add emphasis to a word. The up-and-down inflection of your pitch adds color to your delivery. A single change in inflection may often change the meaning or implication of a sentence. "How dare you use that tone of voice on me!"

Example:

I said he was no good.

I **said** he was no good

I said **he** was no good

I said he **was** no good

I said he was **no** good

I said he was no **good.**

Try these exercises.

Always work gently when you do voice exercises. The voice may get tired as do other muscles when you use them, but it should never HURT.

Start on a comfortably low tone and count up the scale as high as you can without straining. Then count back down. Don't "gravel" at the bottom.

Starting at your normal pitch, say "I have a good voice." Repeat three times, getting higher each time. Go back to normal and go lower three times.

Rate:

For almost everyone a comfortable speaking rate lies between 130 and 160 words per minute. Speaking too fast can cause poor diction — running words together, slurring words, and dropping word endings — which could result in listeners complaining "What did he say?" A machine-gun delivery can easily lose your listeners.

Your rate should be appropriate for the material. As you know, serious content is going to be paced more slowly than that which is light and upbeat. Be careful not to let yourself get too fast or you'll stumble and get sloppy. You'll also "wear out" your audience.

On the other hand, talking too slowly is just as bad. Actually, it can irritate your listeners even more than talking too fast. When a speaker takes, like what seems, five minutes to draaaaag out a phrase or sentence, she is setting up her listeners to yawn or mind-wander. A sluggish speaker can easily convey an impression of shyness, lack of confidence or intelligence, or illness.

Pacing means an interesting rate of delivery, with enough variation to hold your listener's interest. To describe excitement, you would speed up your delivery. When quoting statistics or emphasizing several points, you would slow down your pace. Speaking at a constant rate, either fast or slow, can only lead to monotony and loss of your audience.

If you're a "rusher," practice your material very, very slowly. It should feel painfully slow. When you get in front of the audience, you'll probably speed up again, but not to your previous rate.

Practice reading stories at an obviously "wrong" pace. Read an obituary very quickly, read the results of the 4-H fair very slowly, etc. Then go back and read them at an appropriate rate. This exercise will sensitize you to feeling what is most "right."

Make Use of the Dramatic Pause: Pauses keep listeners in suspense and add variety, excitement and interest to your delivery. We pause for one of four reasons:

- to provide emphasis
- to breathe
- to provide variety in delivery
- to pull your thoughts together

Volume:

Some people have naturally loud or soft voices. If you speak too loudly or softly, your audience will communicate this message to you nonverbally. For example, when you start to speak, do they all move back in their chairs as if blown there by a gust of wind? Or do they move up to the edge of their seats turning their ears in your direction?

The size of the room and audience should determine the volume of your voice. If you have a soft voice, start by asking the audience, "Can you hear me in back?" Speaking too loudly or too softly is not only annoying, but it also leads to a breakdown in speaker-listener communication.

Adjust your volume for the situation and make sure you aren't relying on the microphone for the energy that should come from your voice. It's easy to get too "laid-back" when you're seated, so even your practice sessions should be done standing. In a public speech try to rehearse with the amplification system. Listeners don't want to be shouted at, but they get irritated when they can't hear easily.

A strong, resonant quality is the ideal, but sometimes you'll need another sound. Use a variety of vocal qualities to make the characters in your stories distinct from one another and the narrator. The same is true for broadcasters who record promos or commercials. It's important to vary your delivery so that they don't all sound the same. Versatility is key.

Say yes or no in as many ways as you can. Be creative and don't be afraid to be a bit "silly."

Vary your rate, pitch, volume and quality.

For vocal variety practice try reading children's books aloud. Your voice will naturally animate with the story. Record your voice and listen to it resonate in your head for higher vocal tones, in your throat for the midrange and deep in your chest for lower vocal tones. Using more gestures will also help to naturally animate your voice.

Make a list of emotions and attitudes, then say yes or no to express them. Try some other words as well.

Read a news article as different character types: executive, child, sex symbol, snob, etc. Notice how the voice changes. Add some new qualities to your speech and/or broadcast.

It's important to have a balanced, conversational delivery style. Then, there are an infinite number of ways in which you can use your pitch, rate, volume and quality to add additional interest and variety when the need arises. Enjoy the process.

Maintain Vocal Energy: This doesn't mean you have to shout, but it does mean that you must keep your engine going all the time. Put excess energy into your voice by pitching up, avoiding husky tones and using vocal variety. Release physical tension by engaging your body and using gestures.

Eliminating Verbal Fillers: Avoid using filler words such as "ah", "that is to say", "however", "therefore" as a means of covering silences.

53. QUESTION: HOW CAN I CREATE MORE OPPORTUNITIES FOR MYSELF TO MAKE SPEECHES IN DIFFERENT CAPACITIES?

Answer provided...

You ask about creating opportunities to 'make' speeches. I'm unsure if you are asking how to create opportunities to create i.e. write speeches for others or if you are referring to opportunities for delivering speeches?

I'm going to run with the delivering speeches choice.

I believe there are at least two types of speakers. The first one, using motivational speakers as an example, have one or a few presentations that they become really good at delivering. Many make their living doing so and become known in their field as the 'go to' person.

A second group is what I call 'generalist' speakers. A speaker in this category speaks, generally, in multiple topics of interest to them. I fall into this category.

Your question doesn't address what your level of speaking experience is. If you haven't already and you are over the age of 18, I would whole-heartedly recommend that you join a Toastmasters club if there is one close to you.

You ask about speaking in different capacities. At a Toastmasters club you will learn to speak in the following capacities and probably even more:

- Introducing yourself to a group
- Delivering prepared speeches on a topic of your interest
- Introducing other speakers
- Chairing a meeting
- Answering impromptu questions i.e. Table Topics (topics with no advance warning)
- Speaking according to Parliamentary Procedure
- Debating
- Evaluating another speaker
- Delivering a toast
- Telling a humorous story or telling a joke
- Delivering a report

You will have opportunities to speak within your club, at other Toastmasters clubs and in the public.

You create opportunities to speak by letting the world know that you speak. Here are some ideas that I use to promote myself as a speaker:

- Create a website to post your videos. Here is a link to mine - http://raestonehouse.com/video-presentations
- Create a Facebook Page to promote videos of your speeches
- Write articles about your speech topics and post them to your website or create a blog
- Get followers to your blog
- Link your Facebook Page to your Twitter account to expand your reach
- Create a one-sheet promo of different topics you speak about
- Create a Linkedin profile and add promotional copy about your speech topics
- Deliver stand-alone speeches in the community on topics that would be of interest to a paying audience. I have four

topics related to business communication I run throughout the year.

Participating in a Toastmasters club will expose you to many speaking opportunities and it can be a good way to find out what subject you are passionate about.

54. QUESTION: DISCUSS THE IMPORTANCE OF HAVING AN OPENING STATEMENT IN A SPEECH AND WHY IT IS NECESSARY TO STATE YOUR THREE MAIN POINTS?

Answer provided...

I'm going to take a contrarian perspective and disagree with your statement. There may be situations where you have to take that tact such as defending your thesis but for everyday speeches it would likely be perceived as being boring.

The times are changing and our audience's listening preferences are also changing. We are living in the days of media sound-bytes. Stories have been chopped down to basic elements. Each element needs to serve a purpose to our audience.

I would suggest throwing out the opening statement idea, unless you actually are defending your thesis. You have to grab your audience's attention. 10 to 15% of your speech should be devoted to your opening. You want to set up the rest of your speech.

You want to let the audience know what you are talking about, why it should be important to them and why you are the best person to speak on the topic. You want to grab their attention. Wake em Up, shake em up! As Tom Antion, American Humorist and Speaker promotes.

If you want to put them to sleep, go for the old formula of tell them what you are going to tell them, tell them, then tell them what you told them.

It might work if you are presenting a dry subject at some kind of boring professional symposium, but then again, maybe that's why they are dry and boring...

55. QUESTION: HOW CAN I GIVE AN IMPROMPTU SPEECH?

Answer provided...

You ask a simple question, however providing you a comprehensive answer is anything but simple.

Anybody can give an impromptu speech. Delivering an impromptu speech is simply speaking about a topic you have no warning about and speaking at short notice.

Note that I said *anybody* can do so, far fewer can do it effectively. It takes practice. You have to get used to answering questions and speaking out loud.

If you are over the age of 18, I would strongly suggest you check out Toastmasters. If you have a club in your community, it can be a great place to practice impromptu speaking.

We have something called Table Topics. This is where our Table Topics Master poses a question, usually based on the meeting's theme and puts the question to a specific member to answer.

This gets you up on your feet, thinking fast and responding coherently. Then you will have a fellow member provide you with some feedback on how you did and you can improve. That helps maximize your skill development and your self-confidence when speaking 'off-the-cuff.'

∼

56. QUESTION: WHAT ARE SOME GOOD EXAMPLES FOR PUBLIC SPEAKING?

Answer provided...

Any time that you are speaking to somebody else, you are public speaking.

Many people tend to think of public speaking as standing up on the proverbial soapbox and delivering a stressful presentation to a large group of people.

We public speak almost every day, unless we are a hermit, to the people we meet. We speak to get our needs met. We speak to share our beliefs, our wants and our desires. We speak to others, perhaps, so we don't go crazy.

Public speaking runs the gamut of communicating to one individual at a time or to larger numbers, with or without the soapbox.

I don't know the purpose of this question, but many people identify with having a fear of public speaking. Public speaking takes skills. The same skills we use to speak to individuals can be honed to allow us to speak to larger groups with some extra skills and stage time factored in.

If you have a Toastmasters club nearby and you are over the age of 18, they can be a great way to practice numerous situations that require public speaking. Here are some examples:

- Speaking extemporaneously
- Speaking impromptu (off the cuff)
- Delivering reports
- Delivering prepared speeches/presentations
- Introducing speakers
- Accepting and presenting awards
- Evaluating other member's speeches
- Delivering toasts
- Speaking inspirationally

This likely just scratches the surface of the public speaking opportunities you can get at a Toastmasters club. You learn the skills at your club and you put them into practice in your everyday life.

Public speaking... is speaking publicly!

57. QUESTION: HOW DO I STOP SHAKING WHEN PUBLIC SPEAKING?

In the immortal words of Jerry Lee Lewis "**whole lotta shakin goin on!**".

The 'shakes' are merely a physical manifestation of our nervous energy. It ties into the flight/fight reaction. Our body releases adrenaline so we are prepared to either run away from the stressor or to stay and fight it. In the case of speaking publicly, we are likely staying to fight. By choice! Well, perhaps in most cases.

Not everyone experiences shakes. Equally annoying can be nausea, dizziness, hyperventilation, headache and numerous other somatic complaints. While they are all annoying and perhaps very scary at the time, they serve a purpose. They are designed to keep us safe and out of trouble.

The challenge is in working past these somatic symptoms. In Toastmasters, we often talk about the 'butterflies.' These butterflies are the aches and pains we feel in our stomachs at times like when we have to speak in public. It has probably become a cliché, but it still holds true... the secret is to get those butterflies to fly in formation.

Anxiety isn't necessarily a bad thing. It serves a purpose. When we have it under control, it can give us the energy to deliver a dynamic presentation.

Getting it under control, now there is the challenge.

I started using the technique of imagery in my early years of public speaking and continue to use it to this day. Here are a couple examples. I found I was very nervous when being introduced as the speaker and having to move from my seat to the speaking area. My heart pounded and I would feel the belly butterflies doing the tango.

My solution was to use imagery. As I am waiting to be introduced, I'm processing several things simultaneously in my mind. I see myself going to the front of the room and everybody cheering and applauding me. Whether it ever happens to the degree that I envision it doesn't matter. At the same time, I am rehearsing my opening line and preparing for the energy I need to grab the audience's attention from the opening. I also picture a spotlight on me, with everybody focusing on me. A superstar if you will.

Your mind tends to believe what you think. If you see yourself being successful, your mind will tell the rest of your body to get with the program.

Using imagery in another example, is to prevent the anxiety I experience when I first stand in front of the audience. I help to minimize this anxiety-producing situation by checking out the speaking area in advance. If it is possible, I will go to the speaking area, doesn't matter if the room is empty or not and gaze around the room. I look at where my audience will be sitting, looking from left to right and to the front of the room and to the back. I look to see if there will be any problems with sight lines. Will everybody be able to see me and will I be able to see them?

I also quickly practice my opening lines while there, in my mind. I further use imagery to see myself being successful and the audience hanging on every word I say. If you are going to imagine, might as well make it a good image.

Another technique often recommended to reduce the jitters is to "feel the pain" and do it anyway. Overcoming fear is the same as developing any new skill. It takes practice and lots of it.

Shaking is a physical manifestation of fear. As we become more confident, these symptoms no longer serve a purpose and will eventually disappear. I would suggest acknowledging your shakes are only temporary and it is within you to work past it. Oddly enough the secret to resolving fear is to do more of what creates the fear in the first place i.e. speaking public. Speak often, speak whenever and to whoever you can.

58. QUESTION: WHAT ARE SOME GREAT ATTENTION GETTERS FOR INFORMATIVE SPEECHES?

A nswer provided...

HERE IS WHAT I RECALL AS BEING THE MOST MEMORABLE ATTENTION getter for me. I believe it might have been from an article in the Toastmaster magazine on the subject of grabbing your audience's attention. The presentation was on water conservation.

While holding a glass of water the presenter looked at the glass and then looked at the audience and then took a sip. "This glass of water has gone through eight sets of kidneys before it has collected in this glass. The bad news is that there isn't enough to go around!"

That opening was attention grabbing on several levels.

I often start off with a rhetorical question to engage the audience from the get-go. The idea is to answer the audience's question "What's in it for me?" "Why should I listen to this speaker?" Being that the question is rhetorical, I'm not really expecting an answer.

I'm hoping the audience will be reflective, allowing me to transition to the next stage of my presentation. I also prepare for the eventuality that somebody does actually answer the question and take me in a direction that I don't necessarily want to go. There are a lot of literal thinkers out there that may not realize that the opening question was intended to be rhetorical.

Another attention grabber can be to use a quote that sets you up for your main point. In the past I have delivered speeches on leadership. I have had a good response to "If you think you are leading and you look behind you to see that nobody is following you, then you are just out for a walk. Have you looked behind you lately?"

Tom Antion, author of "Wake'Em Up!" recommends using humor to grab your audience's attention when delivering business presentations, which are likely informative in nature. He also says to use anywhere from 15% to 20% [humor] spread throughout your presentation. If you use humor to grab your audience's attention from the beginning, you can make references to it throughout your presentation or build upon it... or even take it another direction.

59. QUESTION: WHAT ARE SOME TOPIC IDEAS FOR A SUCCESS SPEECH?

Thanks for your question. It's been quite a while since I have delivered a speech on the topic of success. You have fired up my creative juices and I will put creating a speech on success on my 'To Do' list.

There are likely hundreds of ideas you can use for direction if your research quotes on the subject of success. Just take the message from the quote and expand upon it, add your perspective and some examples.

Here are some examples:

"Success is 20% skills and 80% strategy. You might know how to read, but more importantly, what's your plan to read?" -- Jim Rohn. With a quote like this you can go in several directions. The 20-80 formula is known as the Pareto Principal. You could expand upon on that it is evident in almost everything we do. It can be said that "success is 20% inspiration, 80% perspiration."

The quote focuses on the value of reading. Your speech could be crafted around how being an effective reader leads towards success. You could expand upon the how to read to lead towards more success in life. You can expand upon the concept of skills vs strategy. You don't have to agree with Mr. Rohn, you can craft a speech around disagreeing or proving him wrong.

You can look at success from different perspectives.

From the 'over and above' perspective:

"No one ever attains very eminent success by simply doing what is required of him; it is the amount and excellence of what is over and above the required, that determines the greatness of ultimate distinction." --- Charles Kendall Adams

"You don't become enormously successful without encountering and overcoming a number of extremely challenging problems." -- Mark Victor Hansen

"The principle of all successful effort is to try to do not what is absolutely the best, but what is easily within our power, and suited for our temperament and condition." -- John Ruskin

From the 'everyday steps' perspective:

"To succeed in the world it is not enough to be stupid, you must also be well-mannered." – Voltaire

"Some things you have to do every day. Eating seven apples on Saturday night instead of one a day just isn't going to get the job done." — Jim Rohn

"The success you are enjoying today is the result of the price you have paid in the past." -- Brian Tracy

From the 'failure to success' perspective:

"I've missed more than 9000 shots in my career. I've lost almost 300 games. 26 times, I've been trusted to take the game-winning shot and missed. I've failed over and over and over again in my life. And that is why I succeed." --- Michael Jordan

"Behind every success is a succession of failures." -- Rick Beneteau

"Use the Trial and Success method; learn how to improve and succeed by falling and learning from your mistakes." -- Brian Tracy

From the 'never give up' perspective:

"Believe and act as if it were impossible to fail." -- Charles F. Kettering

"All great success and achievement is preceded and accompanied by hard, hard, work. When in doubt, 'try harder.' And if that doesn't work, try harder still!" -- Brian Tracy

"We will either find a way, or make one." --- Hannibal

From the 'secrets to success' perspective:

"Success seems to be connected with action. Successful people keep moving. They make mistakes, but they don't quit." --- Conrad Hilton, 1887-1979, American Hotelier, Businessman, Founder, Hilton Hotels

"How long should you try? Until." Jim Rohn

"The most important single ingredient in the formula of success is knowing how to get along with people." -- Theodore Roosevelt

There are likely quite a few more perspectives that would easily work. As I mentioned earlier, you can agree or agree with the quote and provide examples to back up your view.

Here are some additional ideas that you could use for a speech on success.

- What is the definition of success?
- How do you know when you have achieved success?
- What comes after success?
- How can you be successful in relation to a certain activity i.e. best practices e.g., public speaking, skydiving.
- How do you encourage someone else to be successful?
- How does one model success?
- What works against being successful?
- What are the everyday habits of successful people?

- You could focus on how one highly visible person became successful.
- You could focus on how one average, everyday person became successful.
- You can focus on how small steps, taken every day can lead to large successes.
- You can argue that everyone of us is capable of achieving success.
- Success means win-win, not I win, you lose. Many people are adverse to the concept of competition.

Overall, your speech should be persuasive. You need to convince your audience of the value of achieving success. You need to provide examples of how everyday people overcame adversity to become successful. You need to conclude with a call for action. If you do so, and they listen and follow-up with your ideas, you will have been successful.

Thanks again for your question. Now I have a speech to write...

60. **QUESTION: HOW DO I WRITE A SPEECH ABOUT MYSELF IN THE 3RD PERSON? HOW WOULD YOU START OFF YOUR INTRODUCTION?**

A nswer provided...

INTERESTING QUESTION! OF THE HUNDREDS OF SPEECHES AND presentations I have delivered, I don't think I have ever delivered a speech, in the third person, about myself. As for writing self-promotional copy in the third person, yes, lots of it.

I think one of the initial challenges in creating this type of speech is it is an uncomfortable topic for many of us. Certainly, it is a topic we know more about than any other person in the world, but actually saying it out loud and sharing it with others is challenging. It relies on a certain amount of assertiveness and self-confidence.

Many of us have been told from an early age that we shouldn't talk about ourselves because nobody likes a bragger. I quite often refer to the quote from Walt Whitman, American Cowboy Poet "If you done it, it ain't bragging!"

How you create your speech and the content you include, depends on what your purpose is. Are you speaking to inform, are you speaking to entertain, are you speaking to promote yourself, or is this merely an exercise to get you thinking out of the box?

Let's focus on the 'how would you start off your introduction?' First off, I'm not sure if you are confusing an **introduction** with your **speech opening**. They are very different. The introduction is where you prepare an introduction for your introducer to share with your audience. It should include details that cover who, why, what and how. Why are you speaking? What are you speaking about? Why should the audience listen to you or care about what you have to say? Your introducer is setting you up for success.

There will be times you don't have an introducer and have to fit it into your opening comments. This can tend to take away from your impact.

Your opening on the other hand, should immediately grab the audience's attention and make them want to hear what you have to say. I'm fond of what Tom Antion, an American humor writer recommends about presentation openings "Wake em up, shake em up!"

I have been embracing self-promotion as of late and am writing a book on the subject. If your intent is to share with the world your unique talents, skills, beliefs and values, you can do so in a 3rd person speech about yourself. Once again, your self-confidence comes in to play.

Here is an example of an opening from my Linkedin profile. While not specifically written as an opening for a speech, I have certainly included it in many of my presentations. You will note that I am comfortable at using a tongue-in-cheek style of delivery and am not afraid to laugh at myself.

"How many people can honestly say that they spent part of their formative years in a maximum security hospital for the criminally insane?

Rae can! True, he was working as a staff in the Dietary Department and was able to go home every evening at the end of his shift. Fortunately, that experience hasn't had a lasting effect on him.

Over the past 40+ years Rae has been working as a Registered Nurse, predominantly in the field of mental health/psychiatric nursing. This has provided Rae with an in-depth understanding of human behavior & psychology, which comes in handy for his creative and entrepreneurial pursuits.

Along his life journey he discovered Toastmasters, where he learned the limitations we place upon ourselves are really only our own inhibitions preventing or perhaps protecting us from actions we aren't ready to undertake.

Rae is driven by the creative process and is passionate about turning ideas into reality. As the District 21 Toastmasters District Governor (2007-2008) his theme was "Attitude = Altitude!" He promotes that belief every day in every project he takes on. Ask him how he can help turn your idea into reality.

 As an entrepreneur Rae believes in having multiple opportunities on the go."

It goes on for a little more but I think you get the idea. Not many people would admit to being in a maximum security hospital for the criminally insane and likely don't know anybody who actually has been. It works well as an attention grabber. So, your opening comments should grab your audience's attention and set them up for receiving the message that you want to share.

61. QUESTION: WHAT IS THE IMPORTANCE OF SPEECH COMMUNICATION IN THE BUSINESS SECTOR?

Answer provided...

Whether you are in the B to B (business to business) or the B to C (business to customer) sector, speech communication is important to the success or your business.

When we think of speech communication regarding business, we likely think of having to deliver a prepared speech promoting our business. That is one example, but there are actually many ways being an effective public speaker can enhance your business.

At the basic level, we have our elevator pitches. I recommend you develop a 30-second, 60-second and even ten-minute versions of your self-introduction. These may be delivered to one person at a time, or as part of a larger group introduction. I have likely introduced myself hundreds of times. I was more confident and effective when I had prepared/practiced my pitch in advance.

I have seen countless numbers of people stumble over their self-introductions. We are told not to judge a book by its cover, yet we do it all the time. When we see somebody stumble over their self-introduction, we are left wondering about their credibility and whether they are worth getting to know better. On the other hand, when we hear an effective, enticing self-introduction, we are more likely to be curious or open to speaking to the individual at a later time.

You might have noticed that I mentioned earlier having a 10-minute elevator pitch prepared. If you can't speak for that long about your business and what you have to offer, then who can?

Here is a bit of a twist on that idea. I would recommend that business people create and prepare 4 to 5 presentations. Notice I didn't say speeches. Presentations are where you impart information.

There are likely countless fields of business. Each has its own specialized information that the average person, in this case business owners, is not aware of. I would suggest creating four different presentations of up to 20 minutes in length you can deliver at short notice. That would indicate that you need to do advance preparation. Speaking opportunities do arise at the last moment once people know you are a speaker worth listening to.

Now these four speeches I am referring to aren't elevator pitches. They are not designed to promote how wonderful you are. Well, actually they are, but in a strategic way.

The purpose is to share information that has value to the audience, is interesting and is timely. The idea is to establish the belief you are the local go-to person for information on your particular subject. The last few moments of your presentation is where you add the "Oh by the way... here is what I have to offer or can do for you..."

For example, here are some presentations I am prepared to deliver. All of them are customizable, depending on the requirements of the organization.

Presentations:

- Referral Marketing Works!

- Speaking to Sell
- What Comes After the Elevator Pitch?
- Tagline Tango: Developing Business Slogans & Taglines That Work
- How High Does Your Elevator Go?

Stand-Alone Seminars/Workshops:

- Business Networking 101: The Basics of Networking (title under development)
- Power Networking: Tips & Techniques to Becoming a Power Networker
- How to create an Elevator Pitch that opens doors (title under development)
- Blow Your Own Horn! Personal Branding for Business Professionals

None of these presentations are specifically about my business, but throughout them I interject what I have to offer to the audience.

I would also recommend having a 10 to 20-minute presentation prepared where you do share, educate and promote your business.

As an event organizer, I believe there is a value for businesses to sponsor socially beneficial events. As a sponsor it can be a great way to get your business noticed. As a sponsor I would request the opportunity to speak to the audience. This is a target audience and a great opportunity to thank everyone for supporting the cause, which positions you favorably as well allows you to give a plug for your business.

Another speaking opportunity arises when you become the local go-to-person for the media, when they need an 'expert' opinion on the subject of the day. While you don't necessarily have any control of how they edit the sound-byte, it does give you a good opportunity to be seen as a thought-leader.

I believe public speaking/communicating is an excellent way to promote your business. You need to have the speaking skills and the self-confidence to do so. These are all learnable skills. I also believe that putting yourself out there in the public is a lot like planting seeds. You don't know when or where one of those seeds might grow and present an opportunity for you.

62. QUESTION: WHAT ARE THE BEST TOPICS FOR ENTERTAINING SPEECHES?

Answer provided...

I don't believe that there is a definitive answer to this question.

The best entertaining topics would be determined by the situation and the needs and the interests of the specific group, at a specific point in time.

That might sound confusing! The speech has to be appropriate. For example, years ago at a Toastmasters club humor contest, I heard a young woman as part of her speech ask us "Do you remember when you lost your virginity?" She did and proceeded to tell us about it.

It was funny and definitely an entertaining story. Perhaps in a pub, sharing beers with others, but not in a Toastmasters club. There were family members in attendance. The club President was mortified.

If I was invited to deliver an entertaining speech to a group, I would want to know why the group was gathering in the first place and if there was a theme. Knowing the theme is a good starting point.

I believe entertaining speeches are difficult to craft. What one person finds entertaining, another may not. They may find it offensive. I also believe for a speech to be entertaining, you the speaker need to be a character in the speech. You can tell a story third-person but it adds to the entertainment if you play a role.

I find everyday situations we encounter in life can be entertaining if we put a twist on the story and look at it from a different perspective. Stand-up comics do this all the time. They take situations we all have experienced, interject themselves into the story, doesn't matter if the story is true or not, then twist it on us. We are left unbalanced. That's where the entertainment comes in. We don't know what's going to happen next.

Years ago, I learned a formula that can help create content for humorous and entertaining speeches. It goes PM + T = H (Personal Misfortune + Time = Humor). We all experience situations in life that didn't go as expected or even painfully wrong.

These are the stories we share at family gatherings or perhaps with our fellow workers at coffee break. They could have been very painful at the time they occurred. But with the passing of time and the weakening of our emotions tied into the event, they can be entertaining stories. Adding a message or a learning point to the speech is beneficial.

I also learned long ago, not to let the truth get in the way of telling a good story. The actual event provides the structure of the story. Embellishing can go a long way in making a funny story hilarious.

I would suggest journaling the stories you tell to others. Start off by writing what actually happened, then edit the story by adding the asides, the humor, the teaching points, etc.

Probably the most important factor... is to have fun doing it. If you find the content entertaining, odds are others will as well. Enthusiasm is contagious.

~

63. QUESTION: I WANT TO WRITE A
TWO-MINUTE SPEECH. HOW
MANY CHARACTERS DO I
NEED?

Answer provided...
I think when you refer to *characters*, it would be better to think in terms of *words*.

You are writing the content for a speech, meaning its purpose is to be spoken aloud.

North Americans speak at the rate of 125 to 150 words a minute. If you drop too far below 125, many of your audience will complain. If you boost your rate to 200 or so words per minute, you will likely lose some of your audience. If the speaking rate gets too fast, then it's hard to think about a particular point, when the speaker has moved on to the next.

So, in a two-minute speech, while theoretically, you would need 300 words maximum, based on the above theory, you also need to factor in pauses. Pauses can be built in for dramatic effect or to allow your audience to think about what you have said. If you are intending to be humorous, you need to factor in time for your audience to laugh and perhaps applaud. You need for them to finish before you move on.

I would suggest that you aim at 250 words for your two-minute speech. It goes by quickly!

64. QUESTION: WHAT ARE HUMOROUS TOPICS TO GIVE A SPEECH ON?

Answer provided...

I don't believe there is a master list of topics that would be considered humorous. The challenge is that humor is not universal. What is funny in one part of the world may be offensive in another. Even among people that know each other, one person may find something funny, while another may not.

I try to use humor whenever I can in my presentations. My humor tends to be spontaneous. I find something funny to share in situations as they occur. You might consider it to be situational humor. I find it very difficult to craft a humorous speech.

A formula that I learned long ago for creating humorous speeches is as follows: **PM+T=H. Personal Misfortune + Time =Humor.** These are stories about disasters in our lives, situations that were out of our control and were likely quite stressful at the time. As time passes, our memories fade and we tend to forget the pain and other emotions we experienced at the time. These are the stories we often tell when our families get together, or perhaps at work over coffee. Sometimes we even start to embellish our story so in time they become quite humorous and may even contain a grain of truth.

Some advice I learned from a fellow Toastmaster many years ago was "Never let the truth get in the way of telling a good story!"

Here is an example of PM+T=H in a personal story I often share. Way back in the late 1980s I met one of my long-time wishes and that was to own a motor boat i.e. a pleasure craft. I only owned it for two weeks before I got rid of it. It almost killed me several times in those few short days.

On the first day of owning it I was having troubles starting the motor. I kept pulling on the pull cord and after numerous pulls the engine finally caught. The problem was the engine was in forward gear and shot forward at high speed. I didn't! I shot backwards, landing and sprawling on the cowling of the outboard motor. My face was mere inches from a whirling propeller. It was like getting ready to kiss a food blender! When I quickly recovered myself off of the engine, I found the boat was racing at high speed towards a rock wall. I threw myself over the seats and managed to steer the boat out into deeper water and away from the rocks. Once I got my heart rate back down to normal parameters, I went for a leisurely ride. I didn't tell my wife about this near-death experience for several years.

The next day there was a storm. The boat developed a hole in the keel and sunk to the bottom. I bailed out over 200 buckets of water and left to go get my truck and trailer to pull the boat out of the water. When I returned, the boat had sunk again.

Once on dry land I eventually repaired the hole in the boat, or so I thought! I took my wife out for her first official ride. The hole opened up again and we started sinking. I believed if we took the plug out of the back of the boat, the water should drain out as we moved forward. It should have worked except the engine chose that time to die. We were sinking! I managed to paddle the boat to shore as the water was getting up to our knees, in the boat. My wife was not impressed! Then I hitchhiked home to get the truck and trailer to haul the boat home.

Once again, another repair job. My wife gave me an ultimatum. She wasn't ever going back in the boat and she wanted me to sell it. I had a potential buyer for it, so I took them and my four-year-old son out for a spin. Once again, the boat started sinking. I still recall my young son's words "So I guess they aren't going to buy the boat, eh Dad!" And that is why my wife won't let me buy a boat...

At the time it was extremely stressful. There were several potential death-causing situations. In time, with the addition of physical humor while delivering the speech, such as throwing myself across the engine when it took off and then throwing myself over the seats to crank on the steering wheel, it helped add to the humor.

We all have an abundance of memories that weren't much fun at the time but could be extremely funny now that we aren't attached to the original emotions. Stories like this can be used to illustrate a point in a longer speech. My example would have fit in well with a speech on boating safety.

Have fun being humorous!

65. QUESTION: WHAT IS A GOOD PREPARED SPEECH TOPIC?

Answer provided...

There isn't a definitive answer to this question. A good topic for a prepared speech is one that resonates with you. You are passionate about the topic and are compelled to share your story.

That's one side of the equation. The other side is you need to be able to deliver your presentation to an audience that is interested in hearing what you have to say. Your job is to share your passion, so they embrace it as well.

Does that mean if you put your heart and soul into developing and rehearsing a presentation and nobody in the audience likes it, that your speech topic is of no value? Not necessarily. It may mean that you are giving the right speech but to the wrong audience.

Unfortunately, it may also indicate your speaking skills aren't up to the level needed to bring life to the topic. A fabulous topic won't rescue a speaker with poor communication skills.

As for what is a 'good' speech topic it might be helpful to some research. What topics are trending in the news right now? Do you have any experience, or a specific skill set you could leverage and create a speech to showcase your expertise?

Another strategy is to create a personal list of your strengths and your weaknesses. Under the Strengths column, list everything you are good at or subjects you know a lot about. Don't limit your items to your job. Assess every aspect of your daily living. In the Weaknesses column, write down everything you aren't so good at. There is no need to go into great detail, especially if it sets you into a downward spiral of self-pity.

I believe most people will find they have quite a few more strengths than weaknesses and significantly more than they thought they had when they first started. I certainly did when I undertook this personal assessment.

Your list of strengths can be a goldmine for topics for you to speak on. With some research you can even become an expert on a specific subject.

Don't rule out your list of personal weaknesses as a source of good topics to speak about. Odds are, if you are weak in one area, so are many other people. Sharing your weaknesses and how you overcame obstacles can make for a powerful speech topic.

I was terrified of public speaking. After 25 years in Toastmasters I enjoy speaking in public to groups and actively look for opportunities. I've given many presentations on how to improve your speaking skills.

I was crippled by shyness and having to meet and mingle with people at business networking events. So I researched business networking, created my own system and wrote a book on the subject i.e. **Power Networking for Shy People: How To Network Like a Pro.**

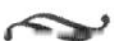

66. QUESTION: WHAT DISTINGUISHES A GOOD SPEECH?

Answer provided...

Simply put, a good speech is one that achieves its purpose. I will add the caveat it is one that has been received by the majority of your listening audience as being good.

As a speaker, we have quite a bit of control as to the preparation, the organization and the delivery of the speech. We strive to be present and in the moment to deliver the best speech that we can, or at least we should be.

We don't have any control as to how the audience, specifically individual members of the audience receive and perceive our message. From our perspective as speakers from the stage, we may see lots of smiling faces that seem to be hanging on every word we say. However, in any audience, there will be people who are not 'in the moment.' They may be focusing on something all-together different. Perhaps a personal crisis going on in their life.

They may even have taken offense at a point or a comment you made and are turning it over and over in their head. The final decision is up to them whether they believe you delivered a great speech, or not.

We see it often in the movie industry. Some critics will absolutely love a movie. Two thumbs up! Others... feel the movie bombed. Three thumbs down! I'm left wondering where that third thumb came from...? It's great, and it bombed! How can that be? Each of us has our filters of likes, dislikes, biases, prejudices and personal experience we use to rate everything we experience in life.

When it comes to my own speeches, I have adapted the view of great, greater and greatest. I've delivered a lot of so-so speeches in my personal journey to hone my speaking craft. I actively work the system i.e. Toastmasters program and my speeches continue to improve. I have been told by some of my audience members that a specific speech was great. I strive to make each speech greater than the one before it. I often deliver the same speech to different audiences and try to incorporate the recommendations made by my previous evaluators.

I believe in the concept of CANEI (continuous and never-ending improvement) promoted by Tony Robbins and Brian Tracy. My greatest speech is sometime off in the future. And likely, I will try to make it greater by doing it again and improving upon it.

I strive for excellence, not perfection...

67. QUESTION: HOW DO I DELIVER A GOOD IMPROMPTU SPEECH?

Answer provided...

Firstly, you need to develop your all-round public speaking skills so when the opportunity arises; you have the *ability* and the *self-confidence* to deliver an impromptu speech. Secondly, you need to say something worth your audience's time to listen to.

Let me clarify impromptu speaking scenarios for anyone reading this response. Here are some examples of impromptu speaking opportunities:

- The scheduled speaker is unavailable
- You are sitting on a panel answering questions from the audience
- You are fielding questions after your own talk
- You are being interviewed on television, radio, webinar, or telephone
- You are invited (at the last moment) to say a few words at a company gathering
- You are asked to provide a brief status report for your project at a department meeting

- You are motivated to join the debate at the parent association meeting for your child's school
- You decide to give an unplanned toast at an event with family or friends

The gist of impromptu speaking is you haven't had the same amount of preparation time as you would for a formalized, prepared speech. At times, it may be a matter of mere minutes.

So, assuming you have the public speaking skills to deliver an impromptu speech, how do we go about crafting one?

Probably, the first task you need to do is ask yourself "Do I know anything about the subject I am being asked to speak about?" There is an old saying that goes "better to keep your mouth shut and let them think you stupid, then to open it and prove you are!"

In most cases you are not obligated to speak other than before a judge in a court of a law or perhaps a grand jury. If you do know something about the subject you are asked to speak about, start writing down your ideas on paper. This is a brainstorming technique.

The idea here is to generate enough ideas to give you something to work with. Then you would analyze your points to see if there are any natural connections between the points. Themes will likely develop as you drill down.

Depending on the amount of time you have for your impromptu speaking opportunity, you may only have time to expand upon one or two of the themes you developed from brainstorming. The next step would be to add personal examples, stories, quotations and facts to add substance to your presentation.

This all presupposes you have at least a few minutes to organize your thoughts before delivering your speech. Often you don't! The same process applies when you don't have the advance preparation time, except you need to do it in your head. This can be challenging.

Once you have taken stock on what you actually know about the question at hand, the next step is to decide on an organizational method i.e. how you will organize your thoughts for delivery.

Here are some organizational strategies to consider. The idea is to practice them in advance of actually needing them, so when the time comes to speak with short notice, you have a variety of tools to choose from.

1. **Compare and Contrast Extremes: (Examples Pros vs Cons/ Negative vs Positive)** Quickly look at any situation from both sides. Create an argument for both sides. This can naturally lead to helping your audience make a decision and increasing your credibility as a 'thought leader.' A conclusion to this strategy is leaving your audience with your recommendations on what choice to make. "Go Ahead Now" versus "Think About It"; "Our side" versus "Their side." Here's a question for you to practice: **Question:** Which are better, cats or dogs as guard animals?

2. **PREP:** Point, Reason, Example, Point. This strategy may be self-explanatory. It is likely the backbone of any speech that you might deliver. The example section is where your personal stories or anecdotes come in handy.

3. **Chronological/Historical (Past, Present & Future)** This is a strategy that can quickly be used to deliver an impromptu presentation of most types. "In the **past...** *this was how things were done...* **currently...** *here is how we are doing it...* but in the **future** *I envision...*" This strategy helps build your credibility with your audience.

4. **Categorical:** Oranges, Apples, Bananas, Pineapples; or Triangles, Circles, Squares, Rectangles; or Customers, Managers, Employees, Sales People.

5. **Hierarchical:** Top, Middle, Bottom

6. **Review Options:** Option 1, Option 2, Option 3, Recommendation

7. **Expanding Radius:** Individual, Neighborhood, Community

Here are some more thoughts on impromptu speaking from Sean K. Michael of Velocity Videos that are worthwhile sharing.

Three Key Ideas:

"I'm content, no matter what!"

Enjoy yourself!

"I can't fail!"

Three Tips:

Tip One: Less is more.

Tip Two: Start with a question.

Tip Three: Make it personal.

Here are even more impromptu peaking tips & techniques:

- Anticipate situations where you may be called upon to speak.
- Wrap your response around a simple template, or framework.
- Turn your impromptu session into a Q&A session.
- Avoid the tendency to go on, and on, and on, and on, and on, and on...

So, I won't... much longer. I would be remiss if I didn't recommend joining your local Toastmasters club to practice and hone your public speaking skills as well as your ability to speak 'off the cuff.' After 25 years as a Toastmaster member I have learned having no knowledge of a subject shouldn't prevent me from being an expert on the subject. Hmmm... perhaps I shouldn't state that publicly ;-)

68. QUESTION AS A PUBLIC SPEAKER, DOES IMAGINING THE AUDIENCE NAKED REALLY HELP WITH ANXIETY?

Answer provided:

No, it doesn't. It is one of those stupid urban legends that have been passed on through the years by well-meaning public speaking instructors.

When I teach public speaking skills, I take an opposite approach. Instead of suggesting that the speaker imagine the audience as being naked... I suggest imagining yourself as being naked!

This totally changes the dynamic. If you are naked, you have nothing to hide. You can be yourself.

There is nothing wrong with being anxious. It is a matter of degree that counts. As you get more comfortable with your nakidity, metaphorically of course, you will become more self-confident as a speaker which in turn will reduce your anxiety.

When I present to a group, I imagine I am in the spotlight. It is my turn to shine. I envision being successful, with the group appreciating and being in tune with what I have to say. They want me to be successful as do I.

When I teach public speaking, I usually bring up the concept of looking at your audience as being naked. I tell them it doesn't work and that I think of myself as being naked instead. I then tell them that I'm naked under these clothes, then I make a joke about not focusing on that fact. It's always good for some laughs.

69. **QUESTION: WHAT SHOULD PEOPLE STOP DOING IN THEIR PRESENTATIONS?**

A nswer provided...

Stop:

- Being boring
- Reading your presentation
- Delivering lame jokes
- Being sexist, racist, anything that ends in an ist
- Speaking overtime
- Not delivering the goods
- Being condescending
- Speaking too fast
- Speaking too slow
- Speaking too loud
- Speaking too softly
- Not engaging the audience
- Overcrowding PowerPoint slides
- Using copyrighted graphics without permission
- Pacing back & forth
- Not being prepared

- Being unoriginal in thinking
- Repeating what everybody already knows
- Allowing hecklers to take control
- Not answering questions adequately

70. QUESTION: WHAT CREDENTIALS ARE NEEDED OR OF VALUE IN ORDER TO BECOME A MOTIVATIONAL SPEAKER, AUTHOR, AND SPIRITUAL TEACHER?

Answer provided...

Forget about credentials. They aren't necessary to be successful in any of the activities you are asking about.

To be a motivational speaker, you need to develop your basic public speaking skills and then hone them to the point that you are polished, and people want to listen to you.

To be motivational, you need to have first learned a lesson, then be passionate about sharing it with others so they can benefit from your suggestions. This is where the honed public speaking skills come in. You won't be able to motivate anyone if your speaking skills are substandard.

As for being a spiritual leader, I would suspect that you would need to have quite a bit of experience or in-depth knowledge about the particular model of spirituality that you want to promote.

While credentials can help with your credibility, many have gone on to excel in these endeavours without credentials. Credentials don't necessarily guarantee you credibility either. What is important is you walk your talk and provide something worthwhile listening to.

71. QUESTION: DOES MY ANXIETY OVER PUBLIC SPEAKING HAVE ANYTHING TO DO WITH SHYNESS/INTROVERSION, HOW WOULD ONE BEST OVERCOME THIS INTENSE ANXIETY?

A
nswer provided...

You are asking about three distinct conditions, for lack of a better word.

Shyness, at its root, is basically a lack of communication skills to be able to socialize effectively.

Introversion, on the other hand is where one draws their energy from. Introverts prefer to be alone to recharge their batteries. One can be an introvert without being shy, however it is likely more common that they are.

Intense anxiety when public speaking, is fear-based. For whatever reason, you have become fearful of public speaking.

Can you become less shy and more outgoing... certainly.

Can you become less afraid and more courageous as a public speaker... certainly.

Can you convert from an introvert to an extravert? Not likely. It is the way your brain is hard wired. You can become more outgoing though and still be effective in overcoming the so-called negative aspects of introversion and strengthen your introverted attributes.

As for your 'intense' anxiety, it may not be as bad as you think it is. You have at least a couple choices available to you.

Firstly, you can avoid all public speaking opportunities for the rest of your life. This will certainly reduce your anxiety level, but it may have a paradoxical effect in that you may become even more anxious about the act of avoiding public speaking.

A second option is to embrace your fear of public speaking and do something about it. I did!

If you are over the age of 18, I would suggest that you research on-line to find if there is a Toastmasters club in your community, or close by.

Toastmasters over the past 90 years has helped countless thousands of people overcome their fear of public speaking.

At its basic level, fear of public speaking is related to two components: 1) lack of actual speaking skills and 2) a lack of self-confidence.

The Toastmasters program is a self-paced, self-directed program that will help develop both your speaking skills and increase your self-confidence.

As your self-confidence increases, your intense anxiety should decrease. It will take a while. For some people, it can lower the 'intense' description of anxiety down to a 'manageable' level.

72. QUESTION: DOES PUBLIC SPEAKING REQUIRE IMPROVISATION SKILLS?

Answer provided...

Does public speaking require improvisational skills? No.

Could a public speaker benefit from improvisational skills? Most definitely!

The art of public speaking encompasses many skills. Sometimes it is delivering a one-way flow of information, where the audience is not encouraged to participate or respond.

Other times, it is a two-way dialogue with the audience interacting with the speaker and perhaps changing the flow of the presentation.

One might think of improvisation in the sense of a comedy act created on the spot, with the situation, characters and context provided at the last moment. That is one form.

From a public speaker's perspective, a skilled speaker can adapt to any situation they encounter. It means they can change their content and delivery mid-stream to adapt to changing conditions.

Being improvisational would be an asset to a speaker. One thing to be aware of though is it has the probability of significantly increasing the time of your presentation. If you are only allotted a certain amount of time and you go off script with improvising, it could easily eat up your time.

~

73. QUESTION HOW MUCH SHOULD I CHARGE TO BE THE MC/ HOST AT A MEDIUM-SIZED CONFERENCE?

A nswer provided...

As in many questions, there isn't a definitive answer to this one. It might be more appropriate to ask '*how* should I charge?' rather than '*how much* should I charge?'

You have at least two options for billing purposes: 1) quote by the hour and 2) offer an all-inclusive package.

However, before you do either selection, you need to do an analysis of the event. What exactly is it that you are being asked to do?

And I do mean exactly! There can be a lot of misunderstanding when it comes to hosting an event. Details really do matter.

As the MC/Host, what are the client's expectations? Are they expecting you to stand in front of the room, introduce people and look pretty?

Or are they asking you to either help organize the entire event or take responsibility for organizing just the program part of the event?

Either way, both will take a considerable amount of your time.

Many clients tend to believe they should pay you for the time you are actually on stage, in front of their audience.

Emceeing, is very much like the concept of an iceberg. Much of what has to be done takes place behind the scenes. You need to be compensated for your time.

It is up to you to decide what your billing rate will be. You need to take into consideration and factor in all the operational expenses that it takes to run your business.

Your billing rate will also be dependent on our local market. A larger city may allow you to get a higher rate than a smaller community.

Whether you are being viewed as a commodity or a celebrity Emcee can also affect how much you can charge.

When first starting out in the business, you may very well be in the commodity category.

After you have determined the logistics of the event and what you are being expected to do, I would recommend giving it some thought. Two important questions come to mind. *Can* I emcee this event? And *should I* emcee this event?

I have encountered potential clients where I have determined that I could take on the event but have decided that I didn't want to work with those particular people.

I factor in an informal personality test when considering events to take on. If the client is agitated, critical or demanding in the price negotiation phase, they will likely continue to be so when you are working with them. Unless I was absolutely desperate for money, I wouldn't work with them.

74. QUESTION: I WANT TO BE HEARD. WHAT DO I DO?

Answer provided...

Just because you feel you have lots of things to talk about and you want lots of people to hear what you say does not necessarily mean lots of people or any at all will want to hear what you have to say.

Those are some hard facts. Your audience is interested in hearing what is important to them. If you are not sharing something with them of value to them, they will filter you out.

One of the first requisites to developing a following interested in listening to you is to have well developed public speaking skills. This isn't a one-size-fits-all scenario. There are many types of public speaking situations that require different skills. For example, delivering a keynote presentation is significantly different from facilitating a training session. Both involve public speaking, but the skills used are different.

Once you have your public speaking skills in place, you need to develop your reputation as a speaker. It is recommended that you specialize in a few topics rather than being a generalist.

Writing goes hand in hand with speaking. You would be well-advised to write articles to accompany whatever it is you feel the need to speak about and share with others. Your written content can easily be cross-promoted over different on-line venues including a blog and posting on Quora. You might want to consider expanding upon your Quora responses i.e. provide more thought and detail.

The more you speak in public and publish your ideas the better the chance you will be noticed. The idea is to become the 'go to' person on a specific topic.

A great way to put all this together, assuming you are over the age of 18 is to join a local Toastmasters club. There you will have ample opportunities to hone your public speaking skills and practice the messages you want to get across to others.

Video recording your presentations and posting them on-line can be a good way to build your audience and perhaps create some speaking opportunities for you.

It's worked for me.

75. QUESTION: I HAVE A DIFFICULT TIME SPEAKING LOUDLY ENOUGH TO BE HEARD IN A NOISY AREA. HOW CAN I IMPROVE THE VOLUME OF MY SPEECH?

I don't think the answer should be to learn to speak louder i.e. over the noise. It would seem far better to me to learn to project your voice further. That's not quite the same as speaking louder.

I would also suggest some other strategies. If there is a microphone available, by all means take advantage of it. Learning techniques to grab your audience's attention can be helpful, rather than having to yell over them.

Placing yourself near the centre of control can also help you be heard better.

AFTERWORD

With not having a chance to converse with you the reader, I am hopeful this book was what you had in mind when you purchased it.

In my opening comments I told you this book provides a systematic approach to serving as a dynamic Emcee and that your self-confidence, poise, courage, public speaking skills and courage to take on a role that many others would avoid at all costs, will go a long way in ensuring your success.

Like any other skill, it takes practice. When you do take on an emceeing role, you will make mistakes. Everyone does. The secret is to learn from those mistakes and improve upon them. It has been said that perfection is almost impossible but achieving excellence at what we do is in within everyone's reach.

Good luck with taking charge as the Master of Ceremonies aka Mr. or Madame Emcee.

Rae A. Stonehouse

Author

～

ABOUT THE AUTHOR

Rae A. Stonehouse is a Canadian born author & speaker.

His professional career as a Registered Nurse working predominantly in psychiatry/mental health, has spanned four decades.

Rae has embraced the principal of CANI (Constant and Never-ending Improvement) as promoted by thought leaders such as Tony Robbins and brings that philosophy to each of his publications and presentations.

Rae has dedicated the latter segment of his journey through life to overcoming his personal inhibitions. As a 25+ year member of Toastmasters International he has systematically built his self-confidence and communicating ability. He is passionate about sharing his lessons with his readers and listeners.

His publications thus far are of the self-help, self-improvement genre and systematically offer valuable sage advice on a specific topic.

His writing style can be described as being conversational. As an author, Rae strives to have a one-to-one conversation with each of his readers, very much like having your own personal self-development coach.

Rae is known for having a wry sense of humour that features in his publications. To learn more about Rae A. Stonehouse, visit the Wonderful World of Rae Stonehouse at http://raestonehouse.com.

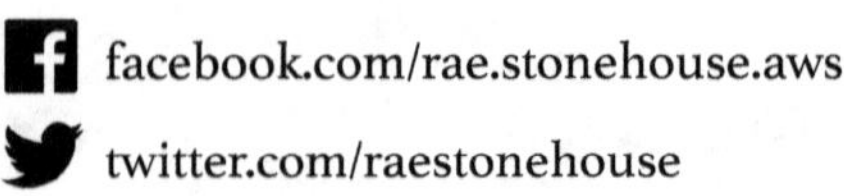

76. ALSO BY RAE A. STONEHOUSE

PROtect Yourself! Empowering Tips & Techniques for Personal Safety: A Practical Violence Prevention Manual for Healthcare Workers https://books2read.com/protectyourself

POWER OF PROMOTION: ON-LINE MARKETING FOR TOASTMASTERS Club Growth

https://books2read.com/powerofpromotion

YOU'RE HIRED! JOB SEARCH STRATEGIES THAT WORK (THIS IS THE complete program)

E-book & Paperback: https://books2read.com/yourehired

On-line E-course: (Available as a self-directed or instructor-led program) http://liveforexcellenceacademy.com/

You're Hired! Resume Tactics: Job Search Strategies That Work

E-book & Paperback: https://books2read.com/resumetactics

On-line E-course: http://liveforexcellenceacademy.com/

~

Job Interview Preparation: Job Search Strategies That Work

E-book & Paperback: https://books2read.com/jobinterviewpreparation

On-line E-course: http://liveforexcellenceacademy.com/

~

You're Hired! Leveraging Your Network: Job Search Strategies That Work

E-book & Paperback: https://books2read.com/leveragingyournetwork

On-line E-course: http://liveforexcellenceacademy.com/

~

You're Hired! Power Tactics: Job Search Strategies That Work **(This is a box set containing the complete content of Resume Tactics, Job Interview Preparation & Leveraging Your Network)**

E-book: https://books2read.com/powertactics

~

Power Networking for Shy People: How to Network Like a Pro

E-book & **Paperback:** https:// books2read.com/networklikeapronetworklikeapro

If you have found this book and program to be helpful, please leave us a warm review wherever you purchased this book.